Four Weeks
To
Finished

How To Stop Making Excuses,
Start Being Prolific,
And Finish Your Novel!

Jake Bible

FOUR WEEKS TO FINISHED

****

*Dedicated to all my readers and all my fellow authors. Y'all
rock!*
*But, mostly dedicated to my family for putting up with my
shenanigans.*

****

Table Of Contents

Chapter One:
Why Am I Qualified To Write This Book?

No matter whether you are reading this as a Kindle sample or standing with the paperback in your hand, before you buy this book, you want to know why this Jake Bible guy (me) thinks he can write about being prolific.

You want the bonafides.

Let's start with the numbers.

Since 2008, I have written fifty-three novels. As of this writing, fifty-one of those have been published, with two of them in the pipeline to be published as soon as editing is done. That's fifty-three novels written in nine years.

Not bad.

Except, that's not the prolific part. The prolific part is the fact that of those fifty-three novels, forty-eight of them have been written since September 2013 when I went full-time as a writer. Everything from *Z-Burbia* and on was written in four and a half years. For the math and stats folks, that means ninety percent of my output has been written during the last half of my professional writing career. That's almost a novel written every single month for the last four and a half years.

Again, not bad.

That's why I'm writing this. The accomplishment of writing a novel in four weeks, which is my output, certainly qualifies as not bad. I've learned a little something about how to be a prolific writer along the way. I have a system that works for me. I stick to my system, and I continue to crank out novels at the same pace, no matter what.

Of course, I wasn't always prolific like this. I had a day job those first four and half years before I went full-time as a writer. You're probably wondering how a book like this can help you when you still work full-time.

Answer: discipline.

Ugh. Crappy answer, I know. But oh so true...

I have the discipline to be prolific, and I am going to share that discipline with you. You may not get a novel written in four weeks because of work and life and everything going on, but you will certainly know how to be the fastest writer you can be.

Oh, and before I forget, I have a couple other bonafides to mention.

I also host a podcast about pro writing called "Writing In Suburbia." Sixty episodes so far. And those fifty-three novels? One of them was nominated for a Bram Stoker Award, which is recognition from my peers that says I not only know how to write, but I know how to write well. Also, every single one of the fifty-three novels I've written has been published by publishers, not indie published. Nothing against indie publishing (seriously, I'm for indie publishing), but it shows that I'm not simply cranking out crap and throwing it on the market so I can call myself a professional.

Every novel I've written has been published.

Bonafides, yo. Bonafides...

By the way, I call this section, and the following introduction, "chapters" so you don't skip them. We all know that everybody skips the introduction, right? Right.

Read on.

Chapter Two:
Writers Don't Make Excuses, Writers Make Stories

As I said before, we all know that introductions in books are usually something readers skim past. Maybe they'll look it over to see if there're any bits of gossip or juicy morsels about the author's personal life. But, really, let's face it, we want to get to the meat of the book and most introductions are lame appetizers that bring nothing to the table.

THIS IS NOT THAT INTRODUCTION!

Why? Because this introduction is your guide to the rest of the book. This little guy helps explain why I repeat points in many chapters, ignore craft questions, and tell you why each chapter matters.

This introduction also explains, in the words you are reading right now, that this book is not a step-by-step guide. I don't know your life. I can't even presume to know what your day to day is like. How can I possibly give you a step-by-step guide on how to be prolific? This book is all about insights, tricks, and tactics I have learned and used over the years to keep writing book after book after book.

Now that you know why this introduction matters, let's get to the actual matter.

Why Be Prolific?

A question I will ask often. It's kind of like Cato in the Pink Panther movies. When you least expect this question, BAM, out it pops! It is a question you need to ask yourself often. You need to be honest with yourself. Why do you want to be prolific? Why do you want to write and finish novels faster? What is your motivation for pushing yourself to your writerly limits?

It's a serious question that requires some self-reflection. Constant self-reflection. It takes a lot out of a person to start and finish a novel in four weeks. It takes a lot out of me to do that and I have the system, the experience, and the time to get it done during the day. I don't write at night (there are exceptions) and rarely write on weekends (again, there are exceptions). Odds are, you will be writing at night, on the weekends, during lunch breaks at work, on vacations, and whenever you can squeeze a free minute from your day.

That's hardcore, and I want to recognize that up front.

For me, the reason I'm prolific is because the publishing industry is no longer a place where a writer can write a novel a year and expect to make anything close to a living. Readers expect product, and they will switch to the authors that provide that product. You and I need to be the authors that provide that product; if we expect to make a living in this crazy business, that is.

None Of This Is Easy

Another bit of wisdom that will be repeated. And it needs to be repeated.

You will read this book and at some point will want to throw it out the side window of a moving vehicle while screaming, "F you, Jake Bible! You suck!" Regardless of the accuracy of that outburst, being constantly reminded that none of this is easy will help you get through the tough parts while also congratulating yourself on the parts that you take to naturally.

We all have our strengths and weaknesses. I have put off writing a "how to" book for a long while despite having a podcast that is basically a "how to" podcast. It makes no sense, I know, but sometimes you get into such a rhythm that doing anything outside your comfort zone and usual pattern can seem so daunting. I certainly have patterns I'm stuck in, especially after writing fifty novels. Just know that what you've been going through with your fiction writing is what I'm going through right now as I write this non-fiction book.

It ain't easy. That simple.

So, don't get discouraged. I'll keep reminding you that none of this is easy and you'll take that to heart, suck it up, and push through. Deal? Deal.

Being Prolific Is About Quantity, Not Quality

More repetitive wisdom!

Yep, I'll be dropping this guy in the chapters, now and again. It is VERY important to listen to and understand; otherwise, you'll get stuck and never finish the damn manuscript.

Here is the thing, folks: quality is subjective.

No matter how hard you try, there will always be people out there that absolutely do not like your writing. I have had more than my fair share of

4

1-star reviews on Amazon that are simply brutal. We are talking middle-schooler behavior vicious. These people bring cruelty to a new level. Oh, well. Nothing you can do about those people.

What isn't subjective is finishing a novel fast. That's finite. Start then finish. Do it all over again. Bam.

You're reading this because you want to know how to be a more efficient writer, how to be disciplined and keep the work flowing, and how to finish a novel then begin on another and another and another.

Getting hung up on quality is just that, getting hung up. You want to be prolific? You need to ditch the idea that every word must be perfect. You need to get rid of that internal editor that is whispering doubt into your mind.

Getting each step done until the novel is finished is all you have to worry about. And this book is designed to take away that worry. Quality? That's for readers to decide. You can't control that. Quality is inefficient and has no place in this book. You can deal with quality after you're done writing and the novel is in the can.

Writing Takes Practice

When I say that writing takes practice, once again, I'm not talking about quality. Yes, the more you write, the better you (should) get at it. Practice makes perfect.

Except the practice I'm talking about is the physical act of writing. Despite all the mental heavy lifting that goes into being a writer, at the end of the day, it is a physical job. No joke, folks. You have to physically put words on paper, or at least put fingers to keyboard, and tell your word processor of choice what to put on the screen. You also have to be in your seat for extended periods of time. Or if you have a stand-up desk, on your feet for extended periods of time.

Like any other physical activity, the actual act of writing takes practice, especially if you are a personality that doesn't sit still well. You have to teach your body how to be comfortable at your writing station. You have to teach your body not to interrupt your mind with twitches and fidget sessions. You have to get used to being in your chair for an hour straight without getting up. You have to teach your body all kinds of things to get through the act of writing.

The more you write, the longer the writing sessions, the more practice you put into the physical act, the more prolific you will become. You'll be able to handle an hour or two in one position. Then you can handle three or four hours. Even if you don't write full-time. Especially if you don't write full-time. If you can achieve the physical state needed to keep your ass in the chair, then when those moments of uninterrupted time occur, they will be used to their fullest.

And, don't worry, I'll give pointers on how to make those writing marathons more comfortable. Writing is physical and takes practice, but it doesn't have to be torture.

Do It Your Way, Find Your Rhythm

Remember this! This is HUGE!

In this book, I will be explaining how I do things. Me. Not you, but me. I can only speak from my experience and about the techniques I've developed to be a prolific writer. They have served me well, but some of them may not serve you the same way.

I want you to keep this in mind as you read this book. I want you to always remind yourself that you are reading this book to help you find your way. If that means copying how I do things, then so be it. But if it means tweaking every bit of advice just enough so that tweaked advice better fits your personality, skill level, and lifestyle, then please tweak all you want.

Part of being prolific is finding your rhythm. It's about finding that sweet spot of efficiency that you can recreate and repeat when needed. You can't be prolific if you try to shoehorn yourself into someone else's rhythm. You'll simply end up fighting the process instead of creating the process.

In the end, this book is about you, not me.

Don't Compare Yourself To Others

This is related to the above point, but slightly different.

You know how you're on Facebook and you see someone having the best time on vacation or out to dinner and you think how nice it must be for them to have all that fun while you're stuck doing laundry? Guess what. They have to do laundry too. They have to clean the toilets and vacuum the house. They simply aren't posting those pics.

It's the same with writing. You watch and read and listen to writers talk about their triumphs and successes. You see them post about a new contract or finishing a new manuscript. You hear about their books climbing up the charts or getting nominated for awards. You see them being successful and you instantly want to be successful like them.

But you have no idea how they got to that point. You have no idea the trials and tribulations they went through to get there. Hell, it's Facebook, so you don't even know if all that winning is even real! They could be totally lying about a contract or they could be fudging numbers to make it sound like they're more successful than they are.

Don't compare yourself to other writers, is what I'm saying. This is your journey and your journey alone. You can no more be those other writers than those other writers can be you. There is no bar you have to meet. There is no minimum threshold you have to push past to get into the Success Club. All of that is BS.

You are you and only you can be the writer you can be. No one else matters.

This Is A Job!

However, there are some folks you should compare yourself to: laborers.

I'm not joking. Writing is physical, remember?

To be prolific, you have to ignore the art and focus on the work. You must treat writing as a job. That means you make a schedule, you clock in and clock out, you take breaks, you assess your workflow and output, you learn how to balance life with writing, and you hopefully get a paycheck at the end of it all.

It. Is. A. Job.

And if you aren't doing it full-time, then it is a part-time job.

Either way, it is a job.

No way around that, folks.

You Get Out Of This What You Put Into It

I know, I know, some of these points sound like cheesy motivational posters. But the truth is made of cheese. Or not. Whatever.

It doesn't matter how much advice I give, how many points I make, how accurate and spot on my observations are: if you don't put the energy into actually listening to all that advice, all those points, and all the observations, then you won't be the prolific writer you want to be.

Maybe a certain point or bit of advice doesn't make sense now, but once you're neck deep in the process, you might think, "Oh, now I see what he was saying. I got this!"

But if you only half-read this book, or skim it for the "nuggets of wisdom," then you could easily miss an important part that is exactly what you'll need to keep going a month, two months, a year from now.

When being prolific, effort is everything. And you have to put in the effort at every stage.

Say that a couple times.

You are going to have to put in the effort to read this book all the way through and to try to understand as much as possible. If you get frustrated, then ask why. If you think something sounds dumb, then figure out how to make it sound smarter in your own words.

My job is to write this book, your job is to read it. If we both do our jobs, then you'll get out of this book what you want to get out of it. Cheesy motivational poster or not, it's simply the truth.

Only Way To Fail Is To Quit!

Oh, this point will recur a lot in the various chapters of this book. Trust me. You'll probably hate this hunk of motivational hoopla by the end, but your hatred doesn't make it any less true.

And it is something I say to myself all the time!

I still get frustrated, depressed, upset, and full-on rage pissed at times. That's how this job is. Peaks and valleys, ups and downs. You can't avoid the valleys, you can't avoid the downs. They will happen.

Let me stress that: the downs will happen.

The key is to not throw in the towel when you are in a down time.

Didn't hit your word goal for the day? That doesn't mean you quit. You make those words up another day.

You were a week late getting the manuscript done? So? Work on your scheduling better for the next project.

Absolutely hate everything you've written? It happens. Move on to the next project. And the next. And the next.

No one can fire you from writing your novel. Even with a million stumbling blocks, and countless mistakes, no one can stop you from finishing the work. No one can tell you it's all over.

No one but you.

Only way you can fail is if you quit. So don't quit. And if you don't quit, then that means you don't fail. It is completely under your control.

You Will Get Discouraged; Push Through

Notice a theme?

Yes, this point is similar to the previous one, but this one is more nuts and bolts than general philosophy.

The fact of the matter is, you will hate writing. The fact of the matter is, you will think none of your effort is paying off. The fact of the matter is, you are human and humans get discouraged. Writers are humans too, by the way.

You know the trope of the alcoholic writer? Yeah, that's the guy/gal that isn't willing to face the discouragement and push through. They aren't doing the work. They are diving into a bottle and getting all "woe is me!" and, basically, quitting, but doing it in a slow, poisonous manner.

Don't be that guy/gal. Ditch the self-pity, face the ugliness, and keep going. Most of this job is filled with disappointment. If you don't learn how to push through the negative, then you'll never get to enjoy the positive. And, trust me, even with the lopsided ratio, the positive far outweighs the negative.

No Such Thing As Writer's Block

Uh-oh, I've angered some of you reading this. I mean, it is quite possible that half the reason you bought this book is to learn how to get past your "writer's block." And here I go, telling you that what you are dealing with doesn't exist. Screw me, right?

Tough.

There is no such thing as writer's block. I can't guarantee any results from this book other than by the end of it, you'll agree with me that writer's block is a myth.

Is writing hard? You bet. I've said that and will say it again. Remember, none of this is easy.

But writer's block is a choice you make. It is a lie you tell yourself so you don't have to put in the work. I'm not saying it's laziness, I'm saying it is a psychological crutch that people use to justify their fear of...whatever.

9

Get over it, use the tips and tricks I talk about in this book, and just like when you are discouraged and down, you push through. Writers write, people. You put one word after the next and keep doing that until you are done. Don't overthink it!

Hit A Roadblock? Don't Worry, There Are Ideas In Here To Keep You Going

Even though I don't believe in writer's block, I do believe writers hit roadblocks all the time. Roadblocks are real. They are that point in the work where you don't know how to go forward. Maybe you're stuck on a plot point, or you have a character that is needed, but doesn't quite fit. Maybe your right shoulder is killing you from yard work, or you have a bad back and sitting for more than ten minutes is torture. Maybe your kid/parent/loved one is sick or you have to have your house fumigated for critics, I mean, cockroaches.

Life happens, folks. It doesn't stop happening because you want to write a novel. Whether creatively or personally, you will come across roadblocks. This book will have many ideas throughout, geared towards the subject matter of the different chapters, that will help you get past the roadblocks and keep you on the road to being a prolific writer.

Drop The Guilt! No Boohoo!

What I mean by drop the guilt is there is no place in being prolific for beating yourself up over [insert BS reason].

Notice how the last few points have all been about you and coming to terms with the fact that being a prolific writer comes with a whole bag of negatives? One of those negatives is guilt.

Guilt kills productivity.

Want to know a secret? All guilt is manufactured. It isn't real. You have to create it inside you. And if you are putting energy into feeling guilty, then you are taking away energy from writing and getting the job done.

I'm not saying you can't be empathetic to yourself. I'm not saying get a split personality disorder and turn half your brain into a Show Parent, always yelling that you aren't good enough and need to work harder. I'm simply saying that there is nothing to feel guilty about.

10

Maybe you decide to watch Netflix instead of write. Great. You are a human being with human needs. You may want to be prolific, but that doesn't mean you stop being a person that enjoys life. Just do the work and find the balance and it'll all be okay.

But for it to be all okay, drop the stupid guilt over whatever and quit that boohoo crap, will ya?

Temper Your Expectations

You've bought this book. You've read this book. You have done everything I have suggested in this book.

And it still takes you six months to finish the manuscript.

Oh, man, you are bummed! You did what I said to do! You sat your ass down and you wrote! You followed the pointers and advice! You blocked out the world! You carved out time! You didn't quit!

But it still took six months...

Hey, maybe six months is you being prolific. You ever think of that?

I can write a novel in four weeks. It's true. So, that must mean that I write twelve novels a year, right?

Wrong.

My wife is a teacher and I have two kids. That means that my schedule and pattern of work gets thrown out the window during summer and winter breaks. July and August? Yeah, not so productive. December? Forget about it.

That is what I mean by tempering your expectations. Know what you are capable of, build on that, but also keep in mind that the universe is gonna toss you some curveballs. Chaos reigns! You will catch a heavy dose of that chaos. You will.

If you've looked at your life and schedule and think you can write a novel in three months, then maybe be kind to yourself and add a few weeks on to that three-month expectation. Eventually, like I have, you will know how fast you can write when faced with a tsunami of chaos. For me, it cuts productivity by at least thirty percent. That chaos will probably cut your productivity by even more, so keep that in mind.

Temper your expectations, people.

If You Are Gonna Make Excuses Not To Write, Then Writing Is Not For You

Sorry, but I'm going to be blunt here. Not all of you reading this book are cut out to be writers, let alone cut out to be prolific writers.

"I have a full-time job."

"My mother is sick."

"I have a physical disability."

"My car broke down and I lost three days of work so money is tight."

"My computer crashed and I lost all my work."

Should I keep going? Probably not, since I know a few of you are really mad at me right now.

I'm not making light of any of those statements above. They are real and they affect your life and they affect other peoples' lives and they are valid. I see that, I know that, and I empathize with that.

But not one of those statements is an excuse not to write. Not one.

They are roadblocks only and roadblocks can be overcome. Everything can be overcome!

You adapt and figure out how to still write and finish your novel even with all of those occurrences getting in your way. It all goes back to "you can't fail unless you quit." When you make excuses, when you accept those excuses as valid, then you are pretty much gearing yourself up to quit. Don't do that.

Writers don't make excuses, writers get the work done. It may be brutally hard, but writers get the work done. That's what makes them writers.

If you can't get the work done, and insist on making excuses as to why you can't get the work done, then you aren't a writer. I'm not giving you your money back for buying this book, but maybe you should look into something else like tending bonsai trees or learning card tricks.

Writers don't make excuses, writers make stories.

Chapter Three:
The Idea

No matter whether you want to be prolific or only plan on writing one or two novels, it all begins with an idea. In this chapter, I am going to give you tips on picking the right idea, discarding bad ideas (don't do that), what to do when you are stuck for ideas, why it's important to write every single idea down, and a whole lot more.

Having the right idea is not the end-all, be-all of success, but having the wrong idea can certainly hamper your chances at success.

Read on and see why.

Don't Be Overly Ambitious

Odds are, as a writer, you are also a reader. That means you've come across some brilliant story ideas others have written and you are thinking that in order to be successful or to get noticed you have to have the GREATEST IDEA EVER!

While I applaud your ambition, I also feel compelled to tell you that you're in for a world of hurt if you go down that path. We'd all love to have the GREATEST IDEA EVER, but even if you do have the GREATEST IDEA EVER, maybe that idea should be shelved for another day. The whole point of reading this book is to find out how to be more prolific in your writing and getting overly ambitious is one way to kill prolificness before it even gets a chance to grow.

It's this simple: an ambitious idea is going to require more work. More work is not good when it comes to being prolific.

One reason I write so fast is that I'm not overthinking my ideas. I write pulp fiction. Bounty hunters, mercenaries, zombies, giant Godzilla-like monsters, haunted houses, genetically engineered sharks—these ideas are simple and fun. I don't have to do a ton of heavy lifting to make these ideas work. Maybe a little research on weapons or DNA therapies, but in the end, I'm not Michael Crichton. When I write science fiction, it is "soft" science, not "hard" science. I avoid facts and stats. I keep to the characters, the story, and the action. I avoid anything that people can refute.

Keeping your idea simple, at least as you first start trying to be prolific, makes all the difference. Keeping the idea simple cuts down on prep

FOUR WEEKS TO FINISHED

time, which means you can start writing sooner and stay writing instead of double-checking that your story still fits the GREATEST IDEA EVER.

An example is when I wrote *Z-Burbia*. My publisher wanted a "Romero-esque" zombie novel: shambling zombies take over the world and the living have to fight to survive. No twists, turns, or surprises. A straight-up classic zombie novel. I was kind of burned out on writing about zombies, but I needed to write something in order to keep the lights on.

Then the idea hit me. I didn't need to be ambitious at all. Romero's *Dawn of the Dead* was set in a mall and was a satirical take on American consumerism. I live in a suburban subdivision. Instead of a mall, I made the setting my subdivision and the story about dealing with the Home-owners Association. Nothing fancy, nothing complicated, nothing ambitious. I took a classic premise and switched up the setting is all. I also had a lot of experience with dealing with the HOA and what living in a subdivision was really like.

I took the clichéd route and wrote what I knew! No ambition needed.

There Are No Original Ideas

"So, basically, you ripped off George Romero?"

Sure. Why not. I'll own up to it.

Except that I didn't. Did Romero create the genre? Yes, in a way, he did. But even Romero had his influences. Richard Matheson's *I Am Legend* was a huge influence on Romero. Even Romero's original take on the "zombie" wasn't exactly original.

And that's the point I'm getting to: there are no original ideas.

Go ahead. Take five minutes and see if you can think of an original idea. I'm not talking your original idea; I'm talking an idea in a movie, novel, TV show, play, whatever, that was completely original.

Guess what?

You can't.

Because we are all a collection of our influences.

Trust me, the last original idea was when human beings were sitting around the fire in their caves. And even then those story ideas were influenced by the world they lived in.

Have you thought of an idea that is completely original? You have?

No, you haven't. Why can I say that with confidence? Because, when you fail at finding any modern influences, I can say with certainty that

14

the Greeks already did it. Yep. Whether tragedy, comedy, or whatever, the Greeks wrote a play about it.

Still not convinced? Okay, what's your idea? What is it? Oh, how original. Let me point to one of many religious tomes that already have that idea in it. Allegory is a thing, people. Odds are your idea is in one of the great religious works. It's not? Right...

Star Wars was based on *The Hidden Fortress.*

The Matrix is "The Chosen One" myth that every single culture on this planet has. Not to mention the massive influence from William Gibson's cyberpunk novels.

Romeo and Juliet? Try Tristan and Isolde.

Every idea has been tried. Every single one.

But, here's the thing: none of them have been tried and told by you.

Sure, maybe your idea isn't anything new, but the way you tell it will be completely new because only you can tell the story your way. This is why people read romance novels that all have the same basic premise, because each author brings a little something different to their book. Same with mysteries and thrillers. Kid gets kidnapped, detective finds kid. Weapons plans are stolen, super spy has to go get them. People read those books like crazy and never tire of them!

So, don't worry about your idea being original, worry about your writing and your take on that idea being original. That's where it counts.

Do it your way and don't look back.

Write All Your Ideas Down

Oh, I cannot stress this enough!

Write all of your ideas down.

Ideas are what fuel the prolific fire. You can't be prolific without a ton of ideas. So write them down.

You also need to write them down because, let's face it, odds are you will forget some good ones if you don't write them down. Keep a notebook, or use the notepad app on your phone, whatever you have to do to write those suckers down and make sure they are locked in for good.

Even write down the crappy ideas. Write down the ideas you don't think you'll ever write in a million years. Write down the ambitious ideas and the simple ideas. Write them all down. That way when you do need a new idea, you have one at hand and you don't have to go through this process of reading this chapter every time you need motivation for an idea for the next novel.

Also, and this is key, when you write the idea down, you give it substance. You've told your subconscious that the idea matters. Trust me, this will save you a lot of time when it comes to writing the next novel. You already have ideas percolating around in that noggin because you gave those ideas weight by writing them down.

What are you going to do? Write all your ideas down!

Being Prolific Is About Quantity, Not Quality

A couple paragraphs above I say to write all those crappy ideas down. Do it. You will need them too. Hell, eventually, you'll run out of really great ideas and be stuck with crappy ones. Hopefully, by that time, you've got enough writing experience under your belt that you can turn a crappy idea into a great story.

I don't need to beat you about the head with this idea thing, or with the whole quantity over quality thing, either. You get the picture. But as you are holding your nose at writing down a stinker of an idea, just remember that the very core of being prolific is quantity, not quality.

In other words, get over yourself. There is not time to be pretentious when you want to be prolific. Knock it off.

Build up your quantity of ideas starting now.

Hit A Roadblock With Generating Ideas? I Got Some Pointers For Ya

Read books.

Watch TV.

Go to the movies.

Watch a documentary.

Sit in the park and observe humanity. Hell, observe the ducks on the river or lake or pond.

Take a drive and let your mind wander (while still being attentive enough not to drive off the road).

Walk through your neighborhood.

Watch YouTube.

Go to the library.

Meet up with other writers and have a brainstorming session.

16

Do drugs (don't do drugs).

Let the world inspire you. Write those inspirations down.

Still Stuck For Ideas? The Mashup Is The Answer!

I know, I know, I know. It's not so much about coming up with an idea, it's about coming up with an idea that sparks your interest. I get that.

Let me tell you a story. True story. It won't take long.

Before I wrote a single novel, back when I was wanting to be a novelist but hadn't taken those first steps towards actually doing it, I was struggling. I think you know what I mean. I wanted to write a novel. I had the desire and, after months of writing short stories, I felt I had the chops to make a novel happen.

What I didn't have was an idea that piqued my interest enough to get my ass in the chair and keep me there. That part was eluding me.

I had a love for zombie movies, and had read a couple zombie novels, but I didn't want to write the same old zombie story. Ironic, considering writing the "same old" zombie novel would kick off my full-time career as a novelist. But back then, I wanted to do something new and different.

But what?

Now, my one mistake was that I was fixated on the idea that my first novel would be about zombies. No clue why my brain insisted that was how I start my novel writing career. But zombies it was, so zombies it would be.

Then came a revelatory evening.

I was sitting on the couch at night with my wife, watching some TV. The kids were in bed and I was zoning out while fast forwarding through commercials. I went too far and had to backtrack. We've all been there. But, when I stopped the DVR, I'd gone back too far. Ugh.

Except, I'd landed on a commercial for the Transformers 2 movie. I'd always loved Transformers when I was a kid. I had tons of the toys and watched the cartoon religiously. I even had Go-Bots. Fighting robots were a thing I dug. (Still do.)

I stared at the Transformers 2 commercial and something started nagging at the back of my mind. It wasn't the robot-to-vehicle idea, but something else. Seeing the special effects of massive robots fighting and tumbling and spinning in the air triggered a memory. Mechs. Specifically, MechWarrior. That was an RPG that I'd always wanted to play when I

17

was young, but no one would play with me. It's funny how the brain makes connections. From Transformers to Go-Bots to MechWarrior.

Slowly, it hit me. What if I set my zombie apocalypse novel in the future where people used mechs to fight the zombie hordes? Cool. But not cool enough. Mechs stomping zombies could only maintain a story for so long. What was stopping the mechs from total domination over the undead? Nothing. I mean, the only thing that could stop a mech would be another mech.

Which meant...

What if a mech pilot died in his/her cockpit and became a zombie? Would that zombie then be able to pilot the mech and rampage the land looking for fresh meat it could crush in its massive metal hands? Hell yes! That's exactly what that zombie in a mech would do!

And *Dead Mech* was born.

I took two completely different tropes—zombies and mechs—and went all peanut butter and chocolate on their asses. I mashed up two different ideas into one and it was perfect. My mind BURNED to write that novel. I may have brainstormed for a week or so, but not much longer than that. I started writing that novel almost right away and the rest is history.

You see what I'm saying? You probably have ideas, but none of them are lighting that fire under your butt. You think of something like it, but as it sits in your brain, it goes stale. It becomes boring pretty damn quick.

But what if you take two ideas and mash them together? Look at that list of ideas you've been making (you have been making an idea list, yes?) and pick two. Hell, pick three. Can they be combined into one coherent premise? Can you take those ideas and put them together in a way that will not only inspire you to get to writing, but also entertain readers?

Maybe. Maybe not. But have a look at the list and see what's what. I'd be very surprised if you couldn't find two compatible ideas that fit perfectly together.

Personally, I can't wait to see what you come up with.

Look To The Markets!

I'm not saying that you need to write to the market. That can be done, but you're gonna need to have a few novels under your belt first. The reality is that the market moves too fast for you to successfully write for it unless you are already prolific and have a publisher/publishing model that can get your work out to readers fast.

But, this does not mean the market isn't a great place to hunt for solid ideas.

As much as things change, they still remain the same.

There are classics still selling for a reason. There are ideas that readers want to visit over and over again. Find those ideas.

Look at bestseller lists on Amazon of the genres you are interested in writing in. There will be lots of books you have never heard of, but there will also be classics that you have heard of, and probably read, hanging strong with the newbies. Look hard at those classics. Look hard at the novels that are still selling now despite having been originally published years or decades ago. What makes those classics so appealing after all these years?

Now, look at the new novels on those same bestseller lists. What are they about? What elements do they have that push them up the bestseller lists?

What do they have in common with the classics that are listed right next to them?

Ahhhh, there's the key. Right there. What do the old and new have in common?

Find the commonality and there's your idea. Take that kernel that connects the classic with the newbie and build that kernel into something larger. Turn it into your very own idea. An idea that is born out of success since your inspiration was from not one, but two (and maybe more) successful novels.

Like I said, writing for the market takes some practice, but looking at the market for ideas is something you can do right now and it should up your chances of success.

Know Your Audience

Seems self-explanatory, but is it?

I'll go into more explanation later on in the chapter on prep, but you should know now that you need to always keep in mind the audience you are writing for. Mystery readers like things a certain way, so if you plan on writing a mystery, but want to completely explode the genre, be prepared for your idea to possibly fail. Same goes for all the genres.

19

Pick your ideas carefully with that in mind. You may really, really, really want to write splatterpunk and dive into all that gory horror goodness, but that audience will be a lot narrower than the audience for less gruesome horror. Maybe don't start with splatterpunk.

Or, on the other hand, you may already be writing horror short stories and the gorier your writing, the more positive reception you've gotten. Know your audience isn't just about what new readers want, but also what your current readers respond to. Maybe you need to rethink that buddy cop novel you'd intended to write next and dive headlong into the splatterpunk realm since your readers are digging that stuff the most. Variations on a bloody theme may be your breakthrough into being a prolific writer.

No matter what you do, the key is to have that audience in mind when you pick your idea.

Write Only What You Want To Write

Oh, the contradictions you will read!

Yeah, sorry folks, but the publishing world is full of contradictions.

I've been telling you to look at the markets, study the audience, that there aren't any original ideas, yadda, yadda, yadda.

Now I'm telling you to only write what you want to write? Am I the biggest jerk ever or what?

Basically, what I'm saying here is that even though there are no original ideas, that maybe a mashup is the way to go, and you should look at the markets to see what people want, at the end of the day, you are the one writing the damn thing. You could have the greatest idea ever in the history of great ideas, but if you don't want to write the sucker, then your chances of being prolific are close to zilch.

Trust me, I've tried.

I've made the decision (more than once) to write something that I thought the market needed, simply because I wanted to make a quick buck, and my productivity went down the toilet. I wasn't invested in the idea. I was going through the motions to get the job done and it was torture.

Not only was the end result subpar, but I was a little discouraged when it came time to start the next project. Writing something I didn't really want to write took some of that spark out of me. And if you want to be prolific, you need to keep that spark alive.

In short, if you don't want to write something, then don't write it. Ignore everything I've said. Seriously. Ignore me. Move on to the idea you do want to write, even if it is ambitious. You'll get way more done writing what you want to write. And, in the end, the finished product will be something that you, and your readers, will enjoy.

None Of This Is Easy

Hey, have I mentioned that none of this is easy?

Yeah, thought I'd swing by and give you a quick reminder as you try to absorb all this stuff I'm throwing at you. Just when you think you have a handle on the concept of ideas, I toss in some contradictory info and your brain goes sploosh.

Sorry.

But that's publishing.

Part of the trick in this business is to grab the parts that you can relate to and toss the rest away. Start doing that now. Is something I wrote not resonating with you? Then forget it and move on. I'm only giving you advice as I see it. I am NOT the end-all, be-all authority on anything. No writer is, no matter their experience level.

So take a couple deep breaths, remember that none of this is easy, and try to cut through the extraneous crappola so you can get to the stuff that will help you specifically.

Cool? Cool.

Only Way You Fail Is If You Quit

And we are back to this point.

We're only at the end of the third chapter and I may have already discouraged you. My bad.

But to hell with me, right?

That's right. To hell with me. This is all about you. Power through, folks. Get past the frustration and remember that the only way to fail is if you quit.

Not sure about this whole idea generating thing? Move on to the next chapter. And the next. And the next. Those chapters may inspire you. They may contain the advice that you're really looking for. Then come back to this chapter and re-read it. It might make more sense when you have more context on what it takes to be prolific.

Maybe the answer was inside you all the time!

Yeah, I threw up a little too at that motivational poster claptrap, but it's probably true.

Alright, you know what to do (don't quit), so let's move on to some heavy lifting, shall we?

Chapter Four:
The Prep

Wait, prep? As in homework? Ugh! This sucks!

Yeah, well, are you an expert on special forces military techniques? What? You are? Okay, then maybe you've done your prep.

But for the rest of us, odds are we don't have that kind of first-hand knowledge, so we're gonna need to do a little studying.

Also, there are several factors that go into writing a novel fast and not all of them are cerebral.

How's your workstation? Did you eat breakfast? Are you dealing with personal issues? Have you even looked at the market you're writing for? What tense is your novel? Do you have a good backup system in case the power goes out? Do you have enough typewriter ribbon on hand if you are one of those guys that use a typewriter in a coffee shop so everyone is forced to pay attention to you? How long is your novel going to be? Are you going to write an outline or wing it?

All those questions and more need to be at least addressed, if not answered, before you even think of starting the novel. Can you skip all that? Sure. But doing the prep is how I am so prolific. I get my ducks lined up.

Also, the sooner you practice good prep techniques, the sooner you will be doing them automatically in your head. That's a good thing. The end goal of a lot of these processes is for them to be going on subconsciously while you work on your current novel. You write one book while you think about the next book. It isn't easy, but conditioning your brain to overlap projects will seriously cut down your time between novels.

Oh, and as always, don't overthink anything I suggest. Don't get bogged down in the minutiae of it all. Do the prep and move on. You'll get better and faster at prep with more practice.

Did You Get Ambitious With Your Idea? Of Course You Did!

Despite my advice to the contrary, you've probably gotten pretty damn ambitious with your novel idea.

I get it.

I do it all the time even though I know better. Hell, I have an idea for a thriller that is going to take some serious research and prep work. That idea is on the back burner until I have the time to do the work needed to prep properly. In the meantime, I'm writing a sequel to my *Roak* series. Gotta keep the machine moving!

But that's me, not you.

You have gone through all the trouble of coming up with your great idea, and it's the one you want to write, so you'll be damned if you're going to back out now.

Then this chapter is one you'll want to pay attention to. Being ambitious is fine, but it does take more time to execute. Pay attention to the pointers in this chapter and you'll be able to shave off as much wasted time as possible so you get the novel done and can move on to the next one.

Only Way You Fail Is If You Quit, But That's Okay

Wait, didn't I just have this topic only a couple pages back?

Yes. Yes, I did.

But I'm tweaking this one a little to fit the chapter.

You see, sometimes it's okay to quit. That's why I am putting this point at the start of the chapter. If all the prep gets to be too much work and you get discouraged, then I am giving you permission to quit. The idea. Quit the idea. Not writing a novel. Feel free to quit your idea and move on to a different one.

Even if you love the idea, even if it is the novel you want to write, sometimes you have to cut your losses and move on.

Let me give you an example.

I have a novel in my head called *Killer Savant*. Brilliant idea. Original, but still steeped in a genre that people will instantly take to it. The problem is it will take a solid understanding of psychology, as well as private military contracting. I have a little knowledge in both subjects, but not even close to the amount I need to pull off the book.

Simple idea, but a TON of prep work to make it successful. Could I half-ass it? Sure, but it wouldn't end up being the novel I want it to be.

So I have shelved that idea until I have the time to give it the attention it needs to thrive.

I have quit that idea indefinitely.

As you read this chapter, just know that at any time it's totally okay to say, "Screw this galaxy-spanning Sci-Fi idea, I'm going back to basics and writing about an alien invasion in a small town instead!"

Another reason to write all your ideas down and keep them handy. That second idea you had may be needed sooner than you think.

Find Your Motivation

Even if your idea isn't ambitious, even if you love your idea to death, you still need to find the motivation to do the actual act of writing. If you aren't motivated, if you have no real burn to put words on paper, then kick back and wait until you do. I'm not kidding. Don't quit. I'm not saying that (even though I said it above).

No, what I am saying is that you are about to put a lot of work into something, spend countless hours at your keyboard, probably piss off family and friends because you've become a neglectful bastard, and forgotten to feed yourself for the past three days.

For what?

That "what" part needs to be thought out right here and right now. Why are you doing this to yourself and others? Why do you even want to write a novel? Why do you want to become prolific?

Knowing and having that motivation in mind at all times will help you get through the tough parts of being a writer, not to mention giving your life meaning and whatnot.

Know the "whats" and the "whys" before you start.

You Have Your Idea, Your Motivation, Now What? Back To The Markets!

This time, you aren't simply seeing what is on the bestseller lists, you are going to read some of those damn books!

Or, at the very least, you're going to read the free samples available. That works too. Takes a lot less time. But feel free to read entire novels. Up to you and your schedule.

Why do this? Because this goes back to the Idea chapter. Know your market and know your audience. You have your idea, and that is great, but will your idea be embraced by readers? That is hard to predict, but with some prep work, you can at least eliminate some variables that may kill your chance of success from the beginning.

First, you're looking at the quality of the work out there. In this day and age of indie publishing, the reality is that there are a lot of novels that don't quite measure up in the quality department. Does this mean

25

you can let your quality slack? No, but it does mean you don't have to sweat the fact that your prose isn't Hemingway. It goes back to the quantity over quality factor of being prolific.

Second, you can see how other novels in your chosen genre are structured. Do they have three parts with separate chapters within each part? Are they made up of quick scene after quick scene? Are the chapters short or long? Knowing that structure will help you decide whether or not you want to emulate it or go rogue and be completely different. There are bonuses to both approaches.

Third, you'll see what the popular tense and POV of the day is. Are the successful novels written in first person, past tense? Or third person, present tense? You can't predict what's going to be en vogue when you're done with your novel, but you can at least see if there are any specific tense or POV choices that are selling now.

Fourth, you're building your prep muscles on top of muscles you've already conditioned during the idea phase. Repetition is good in this business.

Oh, and also read the reviews! See what readers like and don't like about successful novels. Others' mistakes are good lessons to learn from.

Is This A Series?

"How the hell do I know that? I haven't written the first book yet!"

Hey, no need to yell, I get it. Hard to predict the future.

But, if you are fortune-telling inclined, and know that your idea is probably going to expand beyond one book, then now is the time to get ready for that. You may come across info or details in a specific subject that are cool, but won't work in book one, yet will work in books two and three. Write that stuff down and save it for later. Look at you! You're already getting ahead of your prep for the next couple of novels!

Or, you may think you want to write a series of books then realize that the genre you've chosen doesn't like series. At least not your "trilogy" style series where the main story arc isn't resolved until the last book. Think *Hunger Games* or *Lord of the Rings*, that kind of stuff.

Perhaps readers of the genre you've chosen like series that are made up of stand-alone novels with the same characters. These novels are connected, related, and part of a continuum, but each one contains a story that is resolved within each novel. This is more like your James Patterson, or Lee Child, or Tana French; no grand story arc that takes six books

26

to finish. Nope, you have resolution on the final page and your readers are fully satisfied, but still ready to pick up the next one.

See why I stressed in the last point that you need to know the market and sample some novels? If you've done that prep, then knowing whether or not your idea is a series, and what type of series, will be a lot easier to figure out than if you were going in blind.

Profanity? Decide Now.

Knowing your market pays off again!

Did any of those samples you read have profanity? No? Then pay attention to that.

How about the reviews? Did you take my advice and read some reviews? If you did, then you'll see right off if readers like or hate profanity in the genre.

Let me give you a solid example. Two books, one with profanity, one without.

In Perpetuity is a far-future, science fiction novel that is a mix of *Starship Troopers* and *Full Metal Jacket*. The entire book takes place on the training station *Perpetuity*. This is a training station for space marines. Space marines. Marines. Have I mentioned the station trains marines?

Now, and this may come as a shock to you, but there are some marines, and possibly other soldiers in the various branches of the armed forces, that use profanity liberally. I know, right? Who'da thunk it?

So, in order to give the novel an authentic feel, I sprinkled the dialogue with some profanity. Okay, maybe sprinkled isn't the right word. I might have dowsed the dialogue in profanity. But I was going for authenticity!

Needless, or perhaps not needless, to say that some readers may have taken offense at the offensive language. I get it. Not everyone has a potty mouth. The frustrating part was when some said profanity has no place in Sci-Fi. Uh...huh? Who made that rule?

Doesn't matter. What should have been a slam dunk novel turned into one of my worst reviewed novels of my career. All because of profanity. I do wonder what would have happened if I hadn't used so many F bombs.

Well, I don't have to wonder! Because I wrote a Sci-Fi novel without profanity!

But, since the characters were certainly still military, their dialogue had to have the same cadence as normal, profanity-spewing soldiers would, so I created a euphemism. Instead of the F word, I used Fo. Fo this and fo that.

Guess what? People got mad at that too! Those who actually have served, or currently serve, in the military said it wasn't authentic. Darned if you do, darned if you don't...

But, because the sample that folks could check before buying the book didn't have profanity in it, the novel ended up being my bestselling novel to date. The negative reviews over the fake cursing came well after folks had purchased the book, so sales were never hurt. And there weren't a lot of negative reviews over that subject.

What's the lesson? Sci-Fi readers are freakin' prudes when it comes to cursing. I did not know that going in, but I learned it fast and never made that mistake again. Decide now if you want profanity in your novel and also make sure that the audience won't go all Church Lady on you if you do decide to unleash the curse words.

Oh, and before we go, have you noticed something about this book? In order to make it accessible to everyone, I've kept the language mild. I may have a potty mouth, but maybe you don't. I certainly do not want to offend someone before I have a chance to help them.

I knew my target audience going in, which is everyone, and adjusted accordingly when it comes to the use of profanity. You should do the same.

Write Your Book Description Now. It'll Change. Still Write It Now

Why take the time to write a book description now when odds are the description will change once the novel is finished? Well, I'm glad you asked!

For one thing, it helps focus your idea. That's kind of important. A general idea going in is fine, but as you begin your prep, you need to focus your idea into something more specific. Writing your book description, even though it will probably change, is a great way to fine-tune your idea before you dive into the first chapter.

Another reason to write your book description first is it gives you a peek into whether or not your idea is actually a good one. If you can't write a basic description before you start the book, then how will you be able to actually write the book? I've had a great idea, thought I was ready to get started, then spent hours writing and rewriting my book description until I realized I was about to write the wrong book. I took a step back, tweaked my idea some, then found what the book was truly going to be about. Then I wrote the book description in only a few minutes.

In short, writing a book description up front will save you a lot of wasted time down the road. Do it even if it is hard and a lot of work. Trust me.

Don't Reinvent The Wheel: The Three-Act Structure

Hey, I am all about pushing the envelope and being experimental. I mean, I'm the guy that invented the Drabble Novel. What's that? It's a novel written entirely in 100-word sections. I'm not kidding. Each section was exactly 100 words.

But, being experimental means you are inventing something completely new and different. That takes time, folks. Taking time to be experimental goes against the whole idea of being prolific. Want to write outside the box? Maybe wait until you've got some more skills under your belt. Learn the box before you tear it apart.

I now use the tried and true novel/storytelling method of the three-act structure.

There are books and materials that explain the three-act structure way better than I ever can. But the simple explanation is the first act helps set up the story, the characters, the world the characters live in, and sets the tone of the story. The second act is the meat of the story, with the main character, or characters, being put to the test with the task of solving whatever problem has been set up in the first act. The third act is all about resolution with the climax of the story hitting about two-thirds of the way through the third act.

Set up. Meat. Resolution. The three-act structure.

Now, the beauty of this structure is that it is already known to reading audiences. They have been conditioned to think of stories in this way. Makes your job a little easier when your novel's rhythm doesn't confuse your readers. That's good.

The other great thing about the three-act structure is you can break your novel into three parts and treat each part as its own separate piece. Focus on building and completing the first act. Then when you're done with that, you focus on completing the second act. Then the third act.

You go piece by piece until your novel is done. It will make life much easier when you break up that novel into smaller, more manageable pieces.

This will also help you budget your time when it comes to scheduling your word count goals, which we'll get more into later.

Three-act structure. Use it until you are confident and practiced enough to toss it aside and go your own way. Although, I will say that I haven't strayed from the three-act at all in my novels. Fifty-plus novels using the three-act structure. If it ain't broke, I sure won't be the one to try to fix it.

Outline If You Need To, But Don't Overthink It

In the writing community, there are two types of writers: plotters and pantsers.

I am sure you have heard this. Plotters outline and pantsers wing it.

Those are the only two types of writers out there. The internet has decreed it.

I call BS.

If there are a billion writers in the world, then there are a billion types of writers. Every writer has his or her way of doing things. A billion writers equals a billion processes.

What do I do? I do what the novel calls for. I outline sometimes. I wing it sometimes. I'll wing it until I need an outline to stay on track. Or I'll outline heavily then toss the outline out the window as I get trucking on the novel.

Forcing yourself into one of two camps will severely hamper your productivity. You'll be more concerned on whether you are outlining correctly or whether you are winging it like a boss. Your focus really won't be on the novel, but on what others will think of the process you've chosen. And that's a bunch of crappola.

However, and I'm not telling you how to write (I kind of am), outlining does help. Especially if you aren't quite sure where your story is going to go. Just like with writing your book description down first, outlining will help you get a better understanding of your plot, your characters, and your themes. It'll allow you to play with pacing before you spend countless hours writing chapters that you may not want to use in the end.

So, for the record, I am pro-outline.

To a point.

30

My issue with outlining is that those are words that can be used in the writing of the novel. If you take the time to write a 10,000-word outline, then that is less time to write 10,000 words of story. This means, if you do decide to outline, be brief, be concise, and don't add a bunch of detail and explanation. Details and explanations are for the novel, not the outline.

If you want to be prolific, that is.

If you want to take your time writing your novel, then be my guest, spend two weeks on an outline that is almost a third of your novel's targeted word count.

Like I said, I outline when needed. If you feel you need to, then please do. It does help. Just don't turn the outline into the actual work. It's a tool that assists with the end result; it's not the end result itself.

Write Character Sketches. But, Again, Don't Overthink it

This point is short because it piggybacks on the previous point about outlining.

Go ahead and write some brief character sketches of your main characters. Maybe add in a little dialogue so you know their voices before you dive into writing the novel. Get used to their physical descriptions and personal quirks. This helped me with the flow of my first couple of novels. I even used some of the sketches in the novels, although edited to fit the narrative style.

But, like with outlining, don't overdo this. Your time is best used writing the novel, not creating character sketches. I know it's fun to create characters, which is ninety percent of the appeal of role-playing games, in my opinion, but you've got work to do. Write enough to get to know the characters then get back to the rest of the novel prep.

Super Fast Point On The "Story Bible"

When I do write character sketches or outlines or both, I add them to the same document I have my book description on. This is the beginning of a "story bible." A story bible helps you organize the key elements of your novel. This is very important if you want to write sequels. You already know what characters look like and how you structured the first novel. We're back to not reinventing the wheel here, folks.

First Person Point Of View? Better Know That Character Like You Know Yourself!

Two of my most successful novels have been written in first person point of view. It's a very effective way to write a novel fast. You are pretty much writing stream of consciousness.

Which means you had better know that character intimately.

Z-Burbia is written in first person and the main character, Jace "Longpork" Stanford, is basically an exaggerated caricature of myself. You'd think exaggerated and caricature would be redundant, but when it comes to Jace, it's a pretty apt description. I took all my strengths and amplified them so they'd help him survive in the zombie apocalypse. Then I took all my weaknesses and amplified those for dramatic and comedic effect. *Z-Burbia* was the first novel I wrote in four weeks.

Then there's *Salvage Merc One*, which I call "Jace in space." While Jace Stanford was based off my personality, Joe Laribeau was based off of Jace's personality. Kinda like a copy of a copy. *Salvage Merc One* became my bestselling novel to date. Only problem was that Joe played well in the free sample, but his personality grew old for a lot of readers. The novel sold a buttload of copies, but the sequel tanked.

What was the issue? I didn't know Joe well enough to write him effectively. I simply ripped off Jace Stanford's character and exaggerated his strengths and weaknesses to create Joe. What that did was take character flaws that made Jace human and amplified them so that Joe was annoying. I got lazy and decided to wing it with Joe, thinking I knew him since my idea was to create "Jace in space." Except Joe wasn't Jace, and the series paid for that mistake.

Know your first person POV like you know yourself and make sure every time you go with a first-person narrative that the narrator is fully fleshed out and becomes his or her own person, not just a copy of a copy. My screw up is your learning lesson.

Know That First Scene

This is very important!

I am not kidding here, people. Knowing your first scene before you start writing your novel is integral to writing a novel fast and being prolific.

32

Literally, and I'm using that word correctly here, as I write this chapter, my mind is working out the first scene to my fourth *Roak* book. I sat down this morning to start that novel, which is strange since I rarely write two projects simultaneously, but it's time to get cracking on *Roak 4*. Except my concept for the first scene isn't finished in my head. That's why I'm writing this instead. I can't afford to waste time, so I'm taking my own advice and letting that first scene build up in my subconscious while I work on this book.

I can't stress enough how important the first scene is. That scene sets the tone for the book. That first scene contains the words potential readers see first when they look at a sample of your novel on Amazon. I am more than convinced that some of my books have had slow sales because their first scenes just didn't grab readers enough.

So, while you are doing all the rest of your prep, be thinking on that first scene. Who is in it? Where is it set? What are you telling the reader about the rest of your novel? Does it start in the middle of the action? Or is there some gripping description of a character or setting that pulls the reader in?

Having that first scene formed in your head before you sit down will make a huge difference in your productivity. If I ever get lost during the writing of a new novel, I'll sometimes go and re-read that first scene so I can get back into the headspace that started the whole thing off. It gives me a reset moment and usually puts me right back on track.

Have Research/Reference Materials At Hand

Want to know a real time killer? Having to remember where you saw a certain fact or figure that you need for a plot point or character element. Was it in this doc? On this website? Did I bookmark that website? Wait, am I thinking of a different fact for a past novel? What am I doing?

Part of the prep procedure is to do the research you need to do so you have an understanding of key elements you want to use in your novel. Are your characters geologists? Then you should probably have a book or website at the ready to answer basic questions of geology when you are working on scenes that require knowledge of the science. Don't spend thirty minutes hunting for a fact when you could have it right next to you on a notepad or in a doc on your desktop.

There's another reason to have all your research notes ready to go: the simple fact that it means less chance of distraction. I can't count how many times I have opened up a web browser so I could look up something real quick only to find that I've wasted an hour on social media (which we'll get into later too). How many times have I only needed to know the spelling of a city and ended up answering emails all afternoon instead of writing? Too many times, is the answer to that question.

Keep your workflow going by having the information you need at hand. Don't lose productivity due to disorganization or distraction. Being prepared is an easy fix to a small problem that can balloon into a much bigger one if your discipline slips. Which, inevitably, it will.

Know The Basics

"They're called magazines, not clips!"

Oh, when I heard that criticism, I took it to heart. I had made a rookie mistake in my first novel and used the colloquial term "clip" instead of the technical term of "magazine" when describing the piece of equipment that holds cartridges for certain types of pistols and rifles.

So, what's the big deal? Well, the characters using the term were supposed to be military. Military personnel would never say clip. The second a reader with any knowledge of military terms sees clip instead of magazine is the second that reader is yanked out of the story. You don't ever want that. You want your reader immersed and unable to put the book down.

Make sure you have basic terms down. Make sure your characters use the terms appropriate for their jobs, duties, experiences. A housewife that's never seen a gun in person, let alone picked one up, might use the term clip in dialogue, but in your prose description, you should say magazine.

Regardless of what your "magazine" may be, know the basics now so you don't have to fix them later.

Let's Get Physical! How's Your Workspace?

You've got your research done and handy. You know your first scene. You understand your characters. You are ready to start writing this damn novel!

Slow your roll there, hoss.

How is your workspace set up? This is integral to being productive and prolific.

34

Is your chair comfortable?

Are you facing a window and risking being distracted by nature's shiny stuff?

Do you have a beverage at hand?

Have you eaten breakfast/lunch/dinner/anything?

Is your music queued up (or would it be "cued" up)? Have you chosen music that will help you focus and not cause you to break out into song every couple of minutes?

Have you let the dogs out to pee so they don't come begging to go out just as you have hit a writing rhythm?

These are important things to think about. You are about to embark on a journey. A journey of the MIND! But even though you will be doing some mental heavy lifting, that doesn't mean your body should be neglected. Have a comfortable chair. Pick appropriate music. Eat some food. Get rid of as many distracting elements as you can.

(Bonus bit of advice on choosing music: Video game soundtracks are specifically designed to play in the background, keep you stimulated, but not distract you from your task at hand. I write to a lot of video game soundtracks. Usually ones from the same genre I am writing in.)

Prep your workspace like you are going on a road trip. A road trip OF THE MIND!

Okay, you get the picture.

Backup Your Work!

Sweet bloody hell (yep, I'm cursing with this subject), please tell me you have a backup protocol in place? You better.

Before you type that first word, you need to make sure you have systems set up to save your work as you go. As you go. As. You. Go.

Not when you are done writing, not every few minutes, but as you go. Real time backup.

I lost half a novel because I didn't have the right backup system in place. Lost all that time and effort because of one power surge. I cried. I'll admit it. I cried like a baby.

Now I have my Mac plugged into a surge protector with battery backup. Power goes out? My Mac has time to save everything well before the battery backup runs out of power.

What am I saving to? I personally use Google Drive. It's free. I have a Google Drive folder on my Mac that is the heart and soul of my writing life. Every document, note, video, PDF, book cover, everything is saved there. I can get to it anywhere in the world by logging in to Google. It also saves in real time. I paused for a second to look at this paragraph and the little icon up in the corner of my screen started spinning. That means all the words I just wrote have been backed up. There are lots of other choices like Dropbox or Box, but Google Drive gives me 15GB free and I like free.

Of course, this means I have to have an internet connection. Not everyone has that luxury.

Some of you rolled your eyes at me, but then a lot of you that live in more rural areas know exactly what I'm talking about. No internet means no ability to backup your work to Google Drive or similar services. That's when you invest in backup drives.

Get yourself a flash drive that has a ton of storage and connect it to your computer. For Macs, there is Time Machine, which constantly and continually backs up your entire computer as you work. It's a great feature. If you have a Mac, but don't have reliable internet, then get a backup drive now. As for PCs? There are a hundred software products that are similar. Find one of them, install one of them, use one of them.

Backup your work!

Know The Length Of Your Genre

Knowing the length of your genre is different than knowing the length of your novel.

Before you can begin to figure out your writing schedule, you need to know how many words you plan on writing. But why plan on writing more words than you have to?

By knowing the average lengths of novels in the genre you've chosen then you can more accurately plan your schedule.

You want to write epic fantasy? Yeah, you're looking at well over 100,000 words. You may not be able to get that done in four weeks. Which is okay. In the epic fantasy genre, releasing a book every few months is considered prolific. Let's face it, some epic fantasy authors take years (decades?) to get the next book out.

But what if you're writing a cozy mystery? Then you are looking at a sweet, sweet word count of about 65,000. Basically half the words it takes to write epic fantasy.

Science fiction used to be closer to 100,000 words, but now with the Kindle market dominating the genre, you're looking at closer to 80,000. Again, much better than 120,000 words for epic fantasy.

Thrillers? 90,000-ish.

Horror? 70-90,000.

Oh, but what about age ranges? YA is around 90,000, but Middle Grade is more like novella length and usually under 50,000.

The exception is if you plan on writing predominantly for the eBook market. Which I do.

I write 75,000-word novels mainly in science fiction. I write urban fantasy, horror, and thrillers, too, but I stick with 75,000 words no matter the genre. I have found my rhythm in 75,000 words. I've gotten to the point where I hit 75,000 words every single time. Maybe a thousand or two over, but rarely.

But this is because no one sees the spines of my books. If you plan on having success in the print market, which means your books will be on bookstore shelves, then the thickness of that book better match the thickness of the other books in that genre section. It's a psychological thing with consumers. And readers are consumers. Word count makes much more of a difference in the print market than in the eBook market.

Either way, know the word count lengths of the genres you want to write in. At the very least, it gives you a goal to shoot for.

Give Yourself A Deadline. Give That Deadline A Buffer

You've done your prep and you're ready to get to work. Now what?

Well, part of being prolific is being disciplined, remember? Which means you need to set a schedule and stick to it. You need to create a deadline for yourself, if your publisher hasn't already set one for you, and keep working your ass off to hit that deadline.

The easiest way to explain is by my example.

Like I said before, I write 75,000-word novels. In order to get that done in four weeks, I have to write 25,000 words a week, leaving me a week to edit and revise. 25,000 words a week breaks down to 5,000 words a day, if I work Monday through Friday, which I do. 5,000 words a day means I should try to hit over 1,000 words an hour for four to five hours. This gives me time to eat, walk the dogs, use the bathroom (unless your work chair is a toilet chair then great on you!), and accomplish other stuff that life throws at me on a daily basis.

My schedule is to write 5,000 words every weekday for three weeks then edit those words the fourth week and I'm done. Manuscript gets sent off to the publisher and I start the process all over again. Simple, right?

Nope. I've gotten good, but I'm not so good that I'm immune to all that stuff that life throws at me. Kids get sick. I get sick. Dogs get sick. A plumbing issue happens which means I have to fix the issue or call a plumber and deal with him/her. My wife needs me to pick up supplies for a class project (she's a public school teacher, so this happens often). Power goes out.

Life is chaos, folks. And chaos loves to mess with your deadline.

So, don't just think about how many words you can write in a day, plan on how realistic hitting that word count day after day is going to be. Odds are some chaos is gonna creep into your perfect plan and pee all over it. Prepare for the chaos so you have a realistic and attainable deadline.

Then add a time buffer to that realistic deadline. It'll help psychologically and emotionally to know that buffer is there. Just don't use that buffer as an excuse to slack off when you should be writing, okay?

Don't Compare Yourself To Others

Y'all are looking at that 75,000 word count with a 5,000-word-a-day goal, and thinking that I'm a total jerk for even suggesting you can get that done in four weeks. You have a full-time job. You have a family to take care of. You have a lot of crap going on that will not allow a 5,000-word-a-day goal to be even thinkable, let alone actually possible.

I totally understand.

Yes, the title of this book says you can write a novel in a month, but that's just a title. It's catchy and has a ring to it. And it fits my way of being prolific.

But, you? Realistically, with all you have going on, you'll be lucky to hit a thousand words a day. Which means it'll take twelve weeks or so to be finished. And that is perfectly fine.

Don't compare yourself to me. Don't compare yourself to other writers. My life and rhythm is my life and rhythm. It works for me. What will work for you will be what works for you. You can't be me any more than I can be you.

So, don't start off your novel by being discouraged. Don't read Facebook posts and tweets by authors that have decades more experience and get down because you don't live up. Don't set an expectation you can't meet. And trying to be like someone else is an expectation you can't meet.

Be you and you alone.

The idea of this book is to help you be prolific, but prolific in a way that works for you.

None Of This Is Easy

Overwhelmed yet? Yeah? I get it.

None of this is easy. Even prepping for your novel is hard work. Hell, it's as hard as the actual writing sometimes. But you'll get through it. Step by step, element by element, you'll get through it. And just like the other chapters, the more you practice, the easier it gets.

Don't get me wrong, none of this is easy, and it never, ever will be, but it will get *easier*.

So, more deep breaths. Center yourself and know that even for seasoned pros, none of this is easy. If it was, then everyone would not only write a novel, but they'd be cranking them out at one per month like me, right?

None of this is easy.

Why Be Prolific? Time To Ask Yourself This Again!

Like I say above, none of this is easy, but then again, it doesn't have to be so hard.

Being prolific takes a lot more work than simply writing a novel at a whatever pace and letting it get done when it gets done. This chapter alone on prep is pretty damn daunting, right?

So, time to ask yourself once more, why you want to be prolific. Be sure that fast writing to a fast finish is actually what you want to do. If you are having doubts, then reassess.

It goes back to the "don't compare yourself to others" point. Are you wanting to be prolific because you see other authors cranking out novels? Or do you want to be prolific because you started writing down all your ideas and, damn, if you don't have a lot of ideas and, damn, if you don't want to write at least half of those ideas before you die?

39

Being prolific is not for everyone. Please make sure it's for you before you dive in and then get discouraged. The world doesn't need more discouraged writers. We're drowning in them already!

Write Only What You Want To Write

Reminder number eight hundred and sixty-five.

Write only what you want to write. Just like the previous point, it's time to reassess. You have put a lot of work into this prep, and now you are about to sit down and get to the nitty and the gritty of the actual writing.

Are you sure you're about to write what you want to write? All the prep in the world will not help you if the novel you dive into isn't really the novel that you want to even write.

Reassess before you waste a ton of mental and emotional time.

Are you about to write what you want to write? If the answer is yes, then let's get to the next chapter!

Chapter Five:
The Work

Well, here we are. You have your idea ready. You've done your prep. Now it's time to actually execute. No more planning, no more dreaming, you are going to sit your butt down at your workspace and stay at that workspace for as long as you can.

It is time to write your novel.

In this chapter, I'll drop some hard-earned wisdom on you. I'll explain how I do things and also explain how some of the things I do won't work for you.

This isn't a chapter on craft. I honestly don't care if you use semi-colons or have a prologue. Adverbs? Not my problem. Shifting POVs in the same scene? You do you.

Nope, this chapter is about the work. The actual labor of writing the novel. I'll give you pointers on how to keep at it even when you want to walk away. I'll give you pointers on when to walk away even if you want to keep at it. I'll give you pointers on how to keep from burning out. I'll be giving you all kinds of pointers. Pay attention.

Oh, and for those that need a step-by-step guide, even though I said this wasn't that type of book, there will be my personal step-by-step lists on how I wrote this book and also how I write every novel. But they'll literally be lists, not detailed step by steps. This chapter here is where the details and the meat of the process are explained.

In other words: don't you dare skip this chapter.

And as always, take everything I say with a grain of salt. Adapt and tweak my points to fit your needs and your life. Luckily, even though I have a lot of points to make, they'll be quick and to the, well, point.

Strap in, y'all, it's time to do the work!

None Of This Is Easy

Oh, yes I did! I went there right off!

Come on, folks, a lot of you are freaking out. A lot of you are thinking you barely got through the idea phase and prep phase. Sweet Little Nine Pound Ten Ounce Baby Jesus, how will you get through the actual writing of the novel?

By remembering throughout this entire process that none of this is easy.

None of this is easy.

I've said it before and I'll say it again...

Stay In The F-ing Chair!

The hardest part of all of this? Staying in your chair and writing. I am not kidding. In order to be prolific, you must be at your chosen workstation for extended periods of time. You have to physically type the novel out. And the only way you can do that is if you, wait for it...

Stay in the f-ing chair!

I'll talk about exceptions, needed exceptions, to this point later in the chapter but for now, repeat after me:

Stay in the f-ing chair.

Stay in the f-ing chair.

Stay in the f-ing chair.

Stay in the f-ing chair.

You cannot get the work done if you are not sitting down and doing the work. This is science, people. Also philosophy. With some motivational rah-rah thrown in.

But it's all true.

Stay in the f-ing chair.

Only Way To Fail Is If You Quit

Just throwing this at you real quick before you dive into the labor of writing. You will get discouraged as you come across stumbling blocks with plot and character. You will get discouraged as your butt starts hurting from sitting for three hours straight. You will get discouraged as you work hour after hour after hour and realize you totally missed your word count for the day despite your hard effort. You will get discouraged.

Say it with me: you will get discouraged.

But you can't fail unless you quit. So stick with it. Scream at the world. Scream at the wall. Scream at your dog (don't scream at your dog). Scream at whatever you need to as your frustration boils over.

But do not quit.

Do not quit.

Don't quit.

Find Your Motivation

Yep, I've said this before, but it is way different once you start the act of writing.

All that discouragement above will still be there even if you've made the brave decision not to quit. So, how do you get rid of it?

You remember why you are writing the novel in the first place. You remember why you want to be a prolific writer. You find your motivation.

My motivation to keep going when I absolutely want to do the opposite and curl up in a ball? Money. I have a family to feed. I have a teenage daughter in high school and a son in college. I have a wife that is an elementary school teacher in one of the worst states to be a teacher, in the worst city in the country to be a teacher (Google it).

There are many days that I want to throw in the towel and go dig ditches. I don't mean that metaphorically. I actually think about the bliss of being a real, honest-to-God ditch digger. Then I remember that there will be no future in that profession. Only ditches to keep digging. So, I find my motivation, which is the money I make as a full-time writer, and remember that even though I may be broke now (it happens), being a writer offers me a possible future of wealth and comfort.

As long as I don't quit.

Ha! See what I did there? Throwback to the previous point! Bam!

In order to keep going, you have to find your own motivation. Know it now so you can grab ahold of it later when you are ready to quit. Find that motivation because it will be your life preserver as you get bogged down in the work of writing the novel.

Hit Your Word Count Every Day. But Don't Kill Yourself

You are ready to get down to the brass tacks of writing.

You've sat your butt in your chair, you've stayed sitting, and you are writing the novel!

Huzzah!

Now keep writing. You created a schedule, and you divided your word count goal into manageable chunks based on what you know you can accomplish within the parameters of your lifestyle.

So, hit that word count. Just do it. Do it.

And, on some days, preferably most days, you will hit your word count. You'll get into your creative rhythm and all those words will come pouring out of you. These are great days. These are the days you rely on to be prolific and get this novel done.

But, for Isaac Asimov's sake, don't kill yourself. Especially not over a word count or a novel. It's just a book and, unless there's something going on I don't know about, you are not a slave to your words. For all those days that do work smoothly, you will have days that don't.

You get the words done you can get done for that writing day/session, and that's all you can do. Yes, hitting your daily word count is crucial to being prolific, but you are only human (again, unless there's something going on that I don't know about). What matters is you put in your best effort.

Hit your word count, but don't beat yourself up if you don't.

You're Beating Yourself Up Over Missing Your Word Count, Aren't You?

Stop it. Just stop it. Beating yourself up is the opposite of productive. It's not the end of the world.

But, I've also said that hitting your word count is crucial. Damn me and my contradictory ways!

Except they aren't contradictory. A word count is a guide, but it is not the novel. Got it? Your word count goals are simply work goals; they are not what makes up your novel. Sometimes you have to backtrack, sometimes you have to rewrite, sometimes you realize your research is flawed. This all affects your word count.

And sometimes, it all goes so smoothly that you are cranking out words at a pace you've never experienced before. When that happens, you will make up the words. This will happen.

Writing, like life, is filled with ups and downs.

So, you missed your word count for the day? It happens. You'll make it up the next day or the day after that. You'll suddenly have a day free of all distractions and be able to crank out some words. Missing your word count is part of being a writer, and so is making up that missed word count on a different day.

You are not a machine. Don't sweat it if things don't go right every single day.

Remember that thing I said about dropping the guilt? That.

Bank The Words When You Can

This is the other end of the spectrum of word count productivity. Bank the words when you have words to bank.

There will be days where everything goes right. There will be days where your fingers can't move fast enough. You are writing like a fiend and nothing can stop you!

Learn to recognize those days and do not squander them. If you have the time, and the words are flowing, then keep on writing even if you've hit and surpassed your daily word count.

I'm doing that right now.

No, seriously. I've hit my word count for the day yet I am still writing. I'm going to keep writing until my mind shuts down. I know my rhythms and today is a productive day. All the elements are in place to make this one of those days where I get down double what I need to.

It took me a long time to recognize days like this. I used to hit my word count, congratulate myself, and walk away, even though I still had a lot more in me. But, as I gained more experience, I realized these days are few and far between. I need to use them to my advantage when I can.

So, today I am banking words. This means that when I don't hit my word count on a different day, I won't be bummed. I have that word count buffer already saved up. I can miss my word count one day, but treat the next day like a normal work day because technically, I'm not behind.

If the words are flowing, then keep them flowing and bank those words for a rainy day.

The Last Third Should Be A Sprint

Okay, you've stuck with me so far, but I know you have doubts about the whole word count thing. I will now let you in on a little secret.

The last third of the book will be the fastest part you write. At least it is for me.

You see, that first act is all about finding the voice. It's about finding the characters and setting. It's about world-building and getting the readers invested.

Then the second act is when everything you set up in the first act starts to get to work. Setting and character development become story. This is meaty goodness.

But the third act! Oh, the third act! That is when all of the work you've done in the previous two acts pays off. You know who the characters are, you've spent two acts with them. You know your setting, the rules of your world. You know your story! The third act is when you hit that climax and wrap things up. There is no need to invent anything new. No need to start adding to the narrative. You did the heavy lifting in acts one and two. Let the novel carry itself along and simply type, type, type!

Another secret? I never hit 5,000 words a day while writing the first act. Never. I mean, maybe one or two days, but in general, I'm looking at between 1,000 and 3,000 words. For the entire first act. The second act I get a little better and do hit my daily 5,000. But the third act? I'm hitting 8,000 to 15,000 per day.

If you break that down then really, the three weeks of novel writing for me are eighty percent first and second act and only twenty percent third act.

Think of it as a graph. My productivity is at a forty-five-degree angle climb, not a steady plateau. Shoot for that.

Stop Writing Before You Run Out Of Steam

I know, this kind of contradicts the point I made earlier about banking your words. But it makes sense.

I usually stop before my brain runs out of ideas. I stop while I still know what comes next. If I am on a roll and banking words, then I stop when I've written my second to last idea.

For example, I was writing *Mech Corps* and really going at it. I had hit my word count goal and was leaving that number behind. But I knew I was going to hit a wall soon. You can only push so far, so fast. Instead of writing until I didn't know what was happening next, even with an outline, I wrote until I was at the end of a scene then started the next scene.

But I didn't finish that next scene. I wrote just enough that when I sat down at my desk the next day, I wouldn't be lost and could continue. That way, the next day started out productive and I didn't have to work up my momentum. I capitalized on the previous day's momentum.

This isn't just good advice if you want to be prolific. This is good writing advice in general. You'll find lots of authors that suggest this. It's because it works. Get in the habit of doing this and you'll be able to sustain your progress a lot better than if you write until you're spent.

Trust me.

Take Breaks! Exercise!

What more contradictions? Damn you, Jake!

Yeah, yeah, yeah...

Here's the thing, folks, we all need breaks now and again. Sure, keeping your ass in the chair is how you start and finish a novel, but you are human. You need to stand up, stretch, take a walk, eat something.

I structure my day so I have a cup of coffee and breakfast first thing in the morning. I check emails then get to work. I'll work until 12:45pm then I get up, stretch, and take the dogs for a walk down at the park. This helps me work out the physical kinks and knots from sitting at my desk all morning while also clearing the mental kinks and knots.

I usually listen to an audiobook or podcast while I walk the dogs. That helps keep my mind stimulated so that when I get back home and sit down again, I am ready for the second round of writing.

If you can't get out of the house, then think of doing laps. Stand up and walk around your house or apartment. Do a few circuits, find a rhythm, and loosen up a little.

Yes, staying in your chair is crucial, but ending up with a hunched back and muscles in massive knots won't help you at all. You have to take care of your body.

With that said, you should also think about an exercise regimen outside of your writing days. Go hiking on the weekends or walk the city. Take yoga or do Pilates. Maybe a martial art. Your mind is part of your body and keeping your body healthy also keeps your mind healthy.

Not trying to be all hippie-dippy, but diet and exercise play an important role in being prolific. I know if I don't exercise or eat right, then my mind gets muddled and productivity plummets.

Take care of yourself, okay?

The Night Before...

I know I'm not alone when I say that the night before is about as important as the next morning when you are ready to start writing again. I will often go over plot points and other elements of my novel the night before. I don't look over notes, but once I turn out the lights and I'm ready for sleepytime, I think about the work I need to do the next day.

I don't stress and get anxious over the work, just think about it. I let my mind wander as I start to drift off to sleep. If I have an "Ah Ha!" moment, then I will force myself to grab my phone and write it down, but otherwise, I'm simply prompting my subconscious to do a little night-shift work. Let the thoughts and ideas marinate in the back of my mind while I sleep.

This may not work for you. You might need to sit down and write a few ideas before you climb into bed. However you want to structure this part of the process, I do recommend taking only a few minutes each night to prepare yourself for the next day's writing work.

Hit A Roadblock? Let's Get Around That

Uh-oh. You've been doing everything right yet you've still hit a wall. Maybe you can't figure out a character's motivation in a scene, but the scene is crucial to the overall story. Maybe you wrote yourself into a plot corner and can't figure out how to get free. Maybe your plot has veered way off and you don't know whether to backtrack and fix it or keep pushing through.

What do you do?

This is similar to when you hit a roadblock in finding ideas. Take a step back and do something else. You can watch a movie or TV show. Read a book. Listen to a podcast. Work on a different project. Clean the house. Mow the lawn.

If I've gotten stuck, like really stuck, I'll walk away from the manuscript and go watch TV. I try to find a show that is similar in feel to what I'm currently writing. Yes, some people don't like to do that because they're worried the show will influence the current work. I'm not worried about that. For me, watching something that is similar in feel and theme helps give me new ideas. It makes me see things from a different storyteller's point of view. That influence usually shakes things loose in my brain and I can get back to work.

I also cook. I used to do it for a living. Not much of a living, but it was my main profession for years. Cooking is creative and physical for me. It's about coordinating many different elements then bringing them together into one coherent dish. Kind of like how you bring a novel together...

48

I've mentally fixed many a plot issue as I was busy chopping carrots or stirring the soup. If you like to cook, try that.

Or try whatever you like to do. Take a break from writing, but stay active and aware. You'll push through that roadblock eventually.

Still Off Track? Read What You've Written

You've gone for a walk. You've cleaned the house. You've watched TV. You've cooked enough flan to feed the Mexican Army for a decade. (Mmmm, flan...)

Yet, you're still stuck and can't seem to get unstuck.

Time to start at the beginning.

No, no, I don't mean to start completely over. I mean go to the beginning of your novel and start reading.

You'll be tempted to edit as you do that. No need to fight that temptation, although you don't have to edit at that point if you don't want to. I know it saves me time if I fix typos while I'm there. No harm in doing it except for the added time. But that's all beside the point.

The point is, I've lost count of how many times I felt hopelessly stuck then went back and read everything I'd already written and found the answer there. The fix for my plot hole or character motivation was already written; I'd simply forgotten I wrote it.

So, when you get really stuck, re-read your work and see if that kickstarts the brain again.

No Draft Is Perfect! Finish It And Fix It later!

There is a difference between getting stuck naturally and setting yourself up to get stuck.

Remember that you are writing the first draft. First draft. This manuscript isn't supposed to be perfect. Everything isn't going to fit. Odds are, it's a total mess.

That's fine. Let it be imperfect and let it be a mess. That's what editing is for. Right now, your job is to keep writing until you are finished with the first draft. First draft.

Let me say it again: first draft.

First. Draft.

Sometimes You Find The End In The Editing

This piggybacks on the previous point.

You have everything done, but can't figure out the ending. Yes, you took care of the climax, but how do you wrap the full story up?

You don't.

If you don't know how to end the book, then don't end it. Do as much as you can to finish, but leave the ending for the editing (which we'll get into later).

Trust me. I've had this happen more than a dozen times.

I've simply ended the manuscript with issues unresolved then started editing from the beginning. By the time I got to the last chapter, I knew exactly what needed to be done to end the novel because I had a much bigger picture in my head. And most endings need a big picture approach which is hard to do when you are so focused on the inventing and writing.

Sometimes you find the ending in the editing, not in the initial writing, and that's perfectly fine.

Backup Your Damn Work!

Yeah, I feel the need to reiterate this point.

Why? Because literally last week, I was saving my latest manuscript and noticed that up in the corner of the screen, the Google Drive icon was missing. I had no idea how long I'd been writing without a safety net, but I had been.

Double-check your backup procedure and system is working properly. Do it daily. Do it before you start working and once you are done. There's just no reason to take a chance.

Take Notes As You Go

This point could have probably been placed earlier, but I didn't want to distract folks that aren't note takers. I wanted you to focus on the work. Also, taking notes as you write helps more in the editing phase than in the writing phase.

But, hey, every little bit helps, right?

Maybe you create a new character, but realize that he'd have more impact if you briefly introduce him in the first act instead of the second. Write that down.

"Mr. Green in first act."

Or you are in a fight scene and have a brilliant idea for some brutal action, but your main character needs a specific weapon to kick the ass she needs to kick. Write that down.

"Give protagonist super knife in chapter three for fight in chapter five."

Then keep writing! Don't go back and make those changes now. That's why you're taking notes! Once you start editing then you can add those bits or make whatever changes you think you need to make.

Add To Your Story Bible As You Go

In order to create a Story Bible, you need to add information to it.

As you write your novel, you'll want to cut and paste new character descriptions, new objects, new settings and locations, basically any info you might need to remember, into your Story Bible.

In my Story Bibles, I'll have sections for characters, for stuffs (foods, weapons, vehicles), for planets (setting/locations), and even for phrases if I am switching out curse words for euphemisms.

Try to remember to do this as you work. The second you create something new, cut and paste it into your Story Bible. Don't tell yourself you'll go back and do it later. Odds are you won't because you'll be busy. Don't procrastinate. Having that object description on hand can make the difference between keeping your workflow going and coming to a screeching creative halt.

If You Must Research, Then Get In And Get Out

Even if you prepped extensively, there will still be issues that come up. Sometimes you don't discover you need more information about a subject until you get to that point in the story. It does happen. Often, in fact.

So you fire up the Google and type in your search and then you see the Facebook tab and you wonder if anyone has replied to your call for reviews on the last book you published, but you also see that your cousin is spouting his hate all over the screen and you just can't help yourself so you—

NO!

The internet is an evil place! EVIL!

Do not succumb to its evil ways. Get the answer you were looking for and shut that browser down. Get in and get out. FAST!

Which segues into...

Just Freaking Stay Off Social Media While Writing

I'm not saying to stay off for four weeks. No, I'm saying that if you are supposed to be writing, then you have no business checking Facebook or Twitter. Save that for lunch or for the end of the day.

Otherwise, you will get sucked into social media. You will. Try to deny it all you want, but no one is immune.

I will post on Facebook in the morning then set up a bunch of auto-tweets to publish during the day on Twitter. Then I walk away. I'll check social media while I eat lunch. Maybe. Some days I don't even want to, so I ignore the Facebooks and Twitters.

Folks, I have a hate-hate relationship with social media, so I know my limits. Know yours too and never tempt yourself. We all know how much productivity gets lost because you end up taking a quiz or trying to explain to Aunt Mona why her logical fallacies endanger us all.

Just stay off the social media, y'all, okay?

If You're Gonna Make Excuses...

...then maybe being a writer isn't for you.

I have a feeling there is someone reading this book right now and is arguing with everything I've written. Which is totally fine. Like I said from the start, these are simply my opinions and my experiences. They may not work for you. Totally cool.

But, if you are arguing with me because you want to prove me wrong so that you have an excuse not to be productive, so that you have an excuse not to do the work, so you have an excuse not to finish the manuscript, then your issue is way bigger than taking issue with my opinions.

If you are honestly telling yourself that you don't have to put in any of this work, then I don't think writing is for you.

Why? Because writing is hard work and there are no shortcuts. Even this book is no shortcut. I'm giving you advice, not permission to skip out on the work. In fact, I think you know by now that none of this is easy and you have to do the work to get the job done. At no point have I sugarcoated this process.

52

Being a writer is hard. Being a prolific writer is even harder. You get out of this what you put in, remember?

One Last Thing Before We Move On

Life happens. We've covered that.
Sometimes life happens for a really long time. Like days or weeks.
So what do you do if you've had to stop writing for several days? How do you get back in the swing of things?

Just like when you are really stuck, go back and re-read your manuscript from the beginning. Look over any notes you've taken while on hiatus. Then read this chapter from the beginning and remind yourself of what it takes to do the work.

You won't be starting from scratch, but it may feel like it. I've been there. I started a novel at the beginning of December, but then the holidays kicked in and it all went to hell. It wasn't until the first week of January that I could get back to the manuscript. I started from the beginning, re-read my notes, decided I needed an outline from that point on to get me back on track, wrote the outline, then sat my ass down and finished the novel.

It wasn't easy, but nothing about this job is.

Why Be Prolific? One More Time!

Before we move on to the next chapter, you should ask yourself this.
If you still feel like being a prolific author is doable, then great. If you feel overwhelmed, then read the next chapter from the perspective of it being general advice (which a lot of it is) instead of specific advice on being prolific.

You are in control of your career, so do what works for you, okay?
Okay!
Now, how about we get to the chapter on editing?
Ugh. Editing...

Chapter Six:
The Edits

I will admit that the editing stage is my least favorite stage of the writing process. I really, really, really don't like editing. I mean, I finished the damn manuscript, can't it just be over now?

No. No, it can't be over now.

Even though I end up despising my manuscript by the time I'm done editing, it is necessary since, well, you know, readers like things to make sense. Editing is where it all makes sense.

This chapter is going to give you practical tips and shortcuts to make the editing process easier. Use what works for you, discard what doesn't. Although, the vast majority of points I cover in this chapter will turn out to be useful and practical, whether you want to be prolific or not.

None Of This Is Easy!

Just wanted to say it up front. This is probably for me more than for you. I really hate editing, so I have to constantly remind myself that none of this is easy. Seriously. Ask my wife. I grumble about editing for a week.

But it has to be done. So let's do it!

Efficient In Writing, Careful In Editing

Huh?

You're asking yourself if you just opened a fortune cookie, aren't you?

It's simplistic, but true: efficient in writing, careful in editing.

When you're doing the work of writing the manuscript, you can get as messy as you need to. You gear down and get that sucker done. You use techniques to save time and you don't sweat the small stuff.

You are a lean, mean, efficient writing machine!

But that was then and this is now. Now you are an editor, not a writer. That's a totally different hat.

All that time you saved by cranking out your manuscript super fast will now get spent as you carefully, methodically, lucidly go over your work line by line, paragraph by paragraph, page by page. You don't hurry the editing process. You just don't.

Take care as you work through the manuscript. Don't space out, don't edit while watching TV, don't edit while there are distractions around.

Some writers I know actually go to a different physical location to edit. I'll do that at times when I feel bogged down. I pick up that manuscript (if I'm in the red pen phase, more on that later) and I go sit at the kitchen table instead of at my desk. Just being in a different chair can help get me through it.

Slow and steady wins the editing race, okay? Take that to heart.

Alphas And Betas Are Good. Use 'Em If Ya Got 'Em!

Chill. This isn't a chapter on dudebro social hierarchy.

For those that don't know, alpha readers are the first line of defense against you sucking. Seriously. They are the ones you turn to as soon as you finish the manuscript and ask, "So…?" Usually, they are good friends and also writers. People that will give you constructive criticism, but tell you the honest truth in order for you to make those changes that need changing.

Beta readers are your second line of defense. These could still be friends, but usually are your hardcore fans that you trust to tell you which parts of the manuscript work for them and which parts don't. You take their notes and make adjustments to your manuscript, if you feel adjustments need to be made.

Now, if you are just starting out, odds are that your alpha readers and beta readers are the same person(s). You just haven't built up a fan base enough to warrant a dozen readers lined up to devour your words in the timeframe you need them to devour them in.

And here's the tricky part of alpha and beta readers: time.

Personally, I don't have alphas or betas. I don't have the time. I have to get my manuscript written and submitted to my publishers right away so the proofreading can begin and the cover can be designed. I'm small press, y'all. I make my living with volume. The more works I release, the more money I make in quarterly royalties. That's the theory, anyway.

But, if you have the luxury of time and want to use alphas and betas, then you should. They will help you get your manuscript right and they will help you improve as a writer. I'm jealous if you can utilize these fine folks.

Take A Day

This is a big one.

You have finished your manuscript and you are ready to dive right into edits. I applaud your enthusiasm and am glad you are taking the whole hustle of being prolific seriously.

But step back and take a day.

Why? Because you need to let that story sit for at least a day. Hell, some authors let a new manuscript sit for weeks or even months. That kind of timeframe doesn't work if you want to be prolific.

So take a day, let it all clear from your mind a bit, then dive into the edits.

Page Numbers!

You let the manuscript sit and you are ready to get that editing done!

First, add page numbers to your manuscript. Do it now. Don't even bother reading the rest of this paragraph. Go add page numbers.

You back? Cool. I'll explain.

It may seem obvious, but I have forgotten to add page numbers at the top of my manuscript a few times. You don't really need them until it is time to print out the manuscript, but best to get ahead of that now.

Plus, by having page numbers at the top during your first round of edits, you can write down in your notes the page numbers of trouble spots you find. Then you can come back to them and fix later.

Why not fix now? Because you may need to read on before you fix them just in case you already fixed the issues in the story later. It happens. I've edited a scene, thinking that it was a plot hole, only to find out later in the manuscript that I had a plan. A plan I forgot all about in a day. Yeah, your brain will trick you that way.

Put page numbers at the top from the get-go.

Why the top? Because when it comes time to enter red pen edits into the manuscript, you'll be able to see the page number right off instead of hunting at the bottom of the page. For me, that saves time.

Computer Edits Then Print And Get Out The Red Pen

You are going to have a minimum of two editing passes.

The first is on the screen. You scroll to the top of that manuscript and start at the beginning. You will see lots of squiggly red lines from spellcheck. Some are valid red lines that need fixing and some are your word processor not understanding names of characters or planets or simple slang words that are decades old because spellcheck is lame.

I'm kidding. Spellcheck saves my life daily.

So, you read and edit the manuscript once on the computer screen. You hit save. You make sure you added page numbers in the header. Then you print.

Why print? Why not just go back through on the screen one more time?

Because your brain processes what it sees on the screen and what it sees on the printed page in different ways. I am not kidding here. I've tested this theory plenty of times and most seasoned pros will tell you exactly the same thing. So, you print.

Now grab that red pen. Ballpoint. Felt tip. Gel ink. Whatever, as long as it is red. Why red? Because your eyes are instantly drawn to the color red on a white page. Red means warning! You want to make sure you don't miss an important edit when it comes time to enter those edits into your manuscript.

Also, as you find mistakes or make notes in the margins, mark the top of that page with a red X. This will save you so much time later! By marking only pages that have edits on them, you eliminate the need to scan and double-check every single page of the manuscript. You only have to pay attention to the pages with red Xs on top.

Time saver beyond belief!

Once you are finished red-penning the hell out of that stack of paper, enter those edits into your manuscript on your computer and you are done.

Take Notes As You Go

Now that you know what you are in for when it comes to the big picture of editing, let's backtrack a bit and get into some details.

First, you will want to take notes during that first pass (I mentioned this in the add page numbers section). You may not use those notes while you are editing on the screen, but the notes will come in handy later when you are wielding the red pen. It's a good way to make sure your plot is tight and characters are named the same throughout the whole novel.

A great example is when I was halfway through the first pass of one of my *Mega* novels and realized I'd been using "eyes" instead of "eye" when describing a character. Problem being, that character only had one eye. So I made a note of this, and when I went back through the manuscript on the printed page, I corrected all instances of "eyes" for that character. It would have taken me a lot longer to start from the beginning on the screen instead of simply making a note to fix during the red pen phase.

Take notes.

The Effort You Put In Now Will Help Later

Seems self-explanatory, but needs to be said. The more effort you put into your editing now will set up solid editing discipline which you can use and refine with each successive manuscript.

Basically, this means that forming good habits now will payoff later.

Why am I saying this? Because you are in a hurry to be prolific. And humans in a hurry tend to cut corners. You can't cut corners while editing. You have to pay attention, you have to put in the work, and you have to be uncompromising. Start forming this type of editing discipline right away and editing sessions later on will go much, much faster.

Trust me. I hate editing, and I'd hate it even more if I hadn't learned good editing discipline.

Trust Your Gut!

Again, this goes back to being in a hurry.

If your gut tells you that a plot point is wrong, but your head is telling you it's going to take a lot of work to fix, you listen to your gut. Your gut is that inner reader. Your gut is your audience. If you feel something is off, then your audience will feel something is off.

Fix it. Take the time and fix it.

That is the entire point of editing—to catch these kinds of issues and eliminate them so you have a better novel in the end.

Do not slack on this no matter how reluctant you are to add time to your schedule. This is why I put aside a full week for editing. Your gut will speak up and you'll be a fool not to listen.

Don't Throw Away Words

Big truth time: I rarely cut sections out of my manuscripts. Pretty much almost never.

If I have a plot hole or an inconsistency in a character's behavior or something of that sort, I make a note of it during my first editing pass then figure out how to fix it in the second pass.

I do not start chopping out words. Those words are hard fought. Those words are not only hard fought, but they are the whole reason you consider your manuscript done. You've hit your word count.

What I do is find the easiest way to fix the problem. I may add a sentence in an earlier chapter that helps to explain a character's motivation and why her behavior might change. I may add a paragraph or two in the second act so the climax has more emotional punch in the third act. I may even add a whole chapter (short chapter) to act as a bridge between story transitions.

And I might cut some words. But not many! If you can fix the issue by simply deleting a line of dialogue or contradictory description, then do it. If that is the fastest, easiest way to go, then cut those words. If you have to cut a paragraph or two, then do that also, but do it sparingly.

Gotta keep that word count!

You'll Find The End In The Editing

Remember this guy? He's back!

This doesn't happen too often, but sometimes in order to finish the manuscript, you have to leave it without an ending. No worries. After the first editing pass, you will more than likely have figured out how to end the novel. After all, you just read it from start to almost finish. You're in a flow, you have the big picture, and your subconscious has had some time to work it all out.

And, if you've followed my advice, you've been taking notes during the editing process and odds are one of those notes is your solution to how to end the novel.

What happens if you still can't end it? Well, you have a second editing pass to do, so by then, you should be good.

Still can't find the ending? Then take the time to send the manuscript to an alpha reader and ask them their opinion. It eats up time, but you gotta end the novel, right?

Hopefully, the first editing pass will do the trick.

Don't Wait! Dive Into The Red Pen Edits!

When it comes to the time between the first editing pass and the second editing pass, do not take a break. The moment you are done editing on the screen, print out that manuscript and start red pen editing. Do it.

This way thoughts, ideas, plot points, character motivations, all that good stuff, are all fresh in your mind and when you start red pen editing, mistakes you missed before will stand out.

And you will find mistakes!

I am always surprised at how many things I find still need editing even though I just went through the manuscript. Having those printed pages in front of you really does activate a different part of your brain. You see things that you didn't see on the screen.

So, do not hesitate! Print that novel out and get back to the editing!

You Want To Burn Your Manuscript With Fire

It happens. I go through this stage every single time I edit a new manuscript.

The stage? Pure hatred.

I will get halfway through the first editing pass and simply despise the manuscript. I hate it so much. I want to walk away and go watch Netflix and quit this stupid writing gig.

Stupid writing gig...

But quitting isn't an option. Neither is loafing on the couch and watching Netflix.

This is where your discipline is put to the test. Or, at least where my discipline is put to the test. Maybe you won't have the same reaction. I tell myself that it will be different with the next manuscript, but it never is. I end up hating it so much. So, so much.

But I swallow that hate and I power through. I do the work, I get the editing done, I print out the manuscript, I do the work, I get the editing done, then I am actually done!

Hating your manuscript is perfectly natural, just don't let it hang you up or slow you down.

Enter Those Edits

You've finished your red pen massacre of the manuscript. Now get to work and enter those edits into the manuscript on your computer. Good thing you have been marking the pages that need edits, right? Talk about a time saver!

Then, once your edits have been entered, you hit save. I also make a copy of that manuscript and call it "[Title Of Book] manuscript". This way I know the original from the completed, edited version. You may not need to, but it's part of my process.

Just Like With Writing, Editing Takes Practice

I know I sound like Captain Obvious, but it's true. The more you edit, the better you will get at it. I learn something new about my writing every time I edit a new manuscript.

It could be that I realize I use the same phrases from book to book or that I love me some sentence fragments. Whatever it is, the more you edit, the more you start seeing your flaws and your strengths as a writer.

You also get faster at it. You know how to ignore the voice that wants you to run away screaming. You ignore that voice and keep your butt in the chair. You know what music can play in the background and what music is distracting. You learn that maybe the kitchen table is a better editing spot in the house instead of your desk. Or that the local coffee shop has really comfy chairs and they help ease the pain and discomfort of editing.

The more you do it, the easier it gets.

Why Be Prolific? Don't Quit. All That Jazz

Now that you are done editing, how do you feel? Do you want to do this all over again? Like, right now do it all over again?

You're gonna have to if you want to be prolific.

Also, don't quit. Just sayin'. You quit, you fail.

Thus ends my friendly reminders of repetitive advice.

Let's move on, shall we?

Chapter Seven:
The End/The Beginning

This is the wrap-up chapter. All the hard work is done and now it is time to assess your process and take a hard look at this whole prolific writing thing. I'm going to ask you some questions that you need to think about and figure out answers to if you want to keep on this journey of prolific awesomeness. I'll also give you some "what's next?" pointers.

Ready?

This Is A Job

You probably noticed that writing a novel, and especially being prolific, is no picnic.

It's hard damn work!

That's because writing is a job. If you want to be a writer and possibly make a living at it, then you have to recognize that it is a job. Is it art? Sure. But only when the work is finished and you've done your job to the best of your ability. That final product is the art, but the creation of that art is 100% a job.

So treat it like one.

Treat writing like a job and adjust those dreamy expectations you had when you first started.

Show up on time. Do the work scheduled for the day. Do your best work at all times. Take what you are doing seriously.

And don't quit.

Be Thinking Of Your Next Novel While Writing Your Current Novel

This is hard to do, but you'll get the hang of it with some practice.

I am always thinking of my next project while working on my current one. As of this writing, I am thinking of my fourth *Roak* book. I have tons of ideas, and I am letting them all marinate while I write out all this advice for you.

This is another key to being prolific. If you've written down those ideas, then you have a list to choose your next novel idea from. Look at that list often and see if anything grabs you. If an idea does grab you, then let it sit in your subconscious while you work on your current project.

Don't let it get in the way of your current project, though. All you are doing is thinking, letting the next idea hang out in your subconscious mind while your conscious brain works on the job at hand.

Then, when all done with the current project, start everything all over with the new idea. Hopefully, your next project will run a little smoother. I know mine usually does.

Is The Finished Novel Any Good? Who Cares? Move On.

Here's a tough one. Deciding whether or not your finished novel is any good.

Ready for a secret? It doesn't matter. Not yours to decide.

I'm not kidding. It is up to the readers whether or not your novel is any good. Or up to the agents you submit to or the publishers the manuscript is being shopped to.

Your opinion really has zero bearing on what happens next.

Plus, odds are you might not be over the anger of editing and still hate the novel, so do not even try to judge its quality when you have loathing in your heart.

You wrote the bugger. You edited the bugger. You finished the bugger. Job is done! Time to move on and get to the next project and fast. No time for self-pity or wallowing in regret about what you might have written instead.

The novel is done and that's what matters.

Get Back To The Book Description

You have been waiting this entire time for this momentous occasion!

Time to re-read your book description and fix it to fit the finished novel.

By the way, a book description is also called a blurb, cover matter, cover description, back cover copy, and quite a few other names. Call it what you want to, it's what sells your book. Other than the cover.

You now know what the hooks are in your novel. You know the characters, you know the plot. You know the surprises and the reveals. You know that manuscript better than you know yourself. Take all that knowledge and put it into the book description.

63

Well, not all of it. Keep the description concise. Make it exciting by using dynamic words. Let the potential reader know what they are getting into, but leave them wanting more when they are done reading the description.

I'd give you more advice on this, but that description is really going to depend on what your novel is about.

One thing I will say is that you can learn a lot by reading the descriptions of bestsellers. Go to your local bookstore or hop on Amazon and look at format, at words used, look at length. Check out several bestsellers in several genres. Feel free to emulate the description styles that you like. Don't plagiarize, but there's nothing wrong with adapting the style and format of a great book description to fit your novel.

You're Finished, So What Now?

I'm afraid that's up to you and your personal goals. You can send the manuscript off to an agent or you can look into indie publishing. Maybe some small press publishers are having open submission periods. Check those out.

You can also set the manuscript aside until you know what you really want to do with it. That's totally acceptable. As long as you start work on your next novel right away!

Because...

Being Prolific Is About Quantity

Maybe you aren't ready to start shopping your finished manuscript. But if you want to be prolific, then now is when you start writing the next novel.

I will say that maybe taking a few days to decompress from the last novel isn't a bad idea. You don't want to burn out. Take a week and breathe then start at the beginning of the process and get to work.

But don't talk yourself into taking too much time off. Keep the momentum going. You learned a lot with this last manuscript, you want to start the next one while those lessons are fresh in your mind. Otherwise, you'll end up making the same mistakes again and that's gonna hurt productivity.

Finish a manuscript, start a manuscript. That's how this all works.

Temper Your Expectations

This is good advice in general for all steps and stages of a writing career.

Don't expect to knock it out of the park on the first try. Or even on the second try. It could happen, but odds are against amazing success right away.

The odds are also against you becoming a prolific writer overnight. It took me years of practice, as well as suddenly having no day job and lots of time to write, before I could hit my prolific stride. If it takes you six novels or a dozen or two dozen before you achieve your rhythm, then so be it.

Or maybe you do hit your rhythm, but that rhythm produces a novel every three months, not every month. If you can consistently achieve that result, then that's awesome. Seriously. Four weeks to finished is how I work, but it may not be how you work. Your job is to be you, not to be me. At no time do I think everyone can, or should, be as prolific as I am.

Be you and kick ass at being you. That is all I ask.

And, who knows, maybe you'll end up more prolific than I am!

Feel Burned Out? Me Too

Burn out happens. It happens to all of us in this crazy publishing business.

Writing is hard work. It's a job. And, like I have said over and over, none of this is easy.

You followed all the sections, took to heart my advice, found the points that would help you the most, practiced like crazy, wrote that damn manuscript, edited that damn manuscript, now you are an empty shell and don't want to do any of this anymore.

Been there, brothers and sisters. I have been there.

This is when you take an extended break. Despite my advice to dive right into the next project, you aren't going to get good results if you are burned out. You will actually be less productive by ignoring the signs of burnout and trying to push through.

Why? Because burnout work sucks. Odds are you will have to rewrite the majority of what you get done. That's not very productive.

Take a break. Go about life like you did before you wanted to be prolific. Write short stories or don't write at all. Rest your mind.

I've had to rest the ol' noggin more than once. I simply busy myself with other projects until that voice in my head won't shut up about the next novel idea. When I feel the urge to get back in the chair, I get back in the chair and start doing my job.

You're The Boss

I can't stress this enough. You are the boss of you and no one else can tell you how to do your job. That simple. Not one sentence in this book is designed to tell you what to do. Only you can decide what you want to do. All I'm doing is giving advice. Take it, or leave it.

You are in charge of your life, your art, your work, and the future of your career.

You are the boss. There's a lot of responsibility, and accountability, when you're the boss, but there is so much freedom too.

Now, what kind of boss you are is a whole other topic, and not one I plan to get into. That's between you and your therapist.

Time To Seriously Assess

Checklist time. Pros/cons time. Listicle time.

Sit down and go over everything that you endured during this process and take an honest look at each step. Write down what you liked. Write down what you hated. Write down what was confusing or frustrating. Write down what you still don't understand. Write down every little thing you can think of.

Now, go over those lists and see what was/is in your control and what wasn't/isn't in your control.

Family being a distraction is probably out of your control and isn't something you can fix, but maybe you can tweak the less than ideal situation by using earbuds to block out some of the noise.

Maybe that red pen you used leaked through the top page and onto the next page, slowing you down when it came time to enter edits. Get a different type of pen. You can control that.

Maybe your back hurts after two hours of writing. You can get up and stretch more often when writing the next manuscript. Or you might need a new chair.

Did you find yourself spacing off at around 11am? You might need a bigger breakfast or that could be when you walk the dogs. Look at your daily schedule and tweak as needed.

Do your eyes sting at the end of a long writing session? Try lowering the brightness of your computer screen.

Things like the above are what you look at and fix, if needed.

Or don't fix, if it all worked out for you. If you found your rhythm, then lock that baby down and get back to work!

The Final Ask. Do You Want To Be Prolific?

Well...do you?

The pros/cons list and self-assessment should let you know the answer to this question. But maybe you need to try to write a couple more novels as fast as possible before you decide. You might like this process now, but in a year, you could have a completely different opinion.

Keep asking yourself whether or not being a prolific writer is for you. There is zero shame in deciding that taking your time to write novels is how you'd rather work. Being a prolific writer is neither easy nor is it the norm. If it takes you a year to write a novel, you'll have lots of company in this biz.

And there is nothing wrong with that.

Plenty Of Good Advice

Have you decided to slow down and not be prolific? To just let the novel happen organically and not try to race and rush it out of your head?

Cool. Good choice. I actually envy you.

So, what do you do with this book?

The process of writing a novel is still the same, no matter how fast you work. Sit down, write, stay seated, keep writing, and finish the book. That's the job of writing.

Go back through this book and re-read it with your new outlook on your writing process and goals in mind. Take what I say as general advice, which much of it is, and adapt that advice to fit your pace.

Good advice is still good advice and I hope I've given you enough that you will be a better writer after reading this book even if being prolific isn't for you.

Again, None Of This Is Easy And You Only Fail If You Quit

It feels like just yesterday when I told you how none of this is easy and the only way to fail is to quit. It actually could have been yesterday, depending on how fast you read through this book.

But it needs to be said yet again.

None of this is easy.

You only fail if you quit.

Maybe write those down in large letters on a piece of paper and tape it above your desk. Put that paper somewhere you can see it daily. It's a little trick I learned from Benjamin Franklin. Yes, that Benjamin Franklin.

In his autobiography, he talks about certain virtues he wanted to live by. So he wrote those virtues down on paper (parchment?) and tacked those pieces of paper up on his wall. They were visual reminders of the person he was striving to be.

You can create visual reminders of the writer you want to be.

Chapter Eight:
A Quick Interlude Before The Step By Step Examples

I just wanted to say a few things before you move on to my step by steps on how I start, write, and finish a novel, plus the step by step on how I created this book you are currently reading. Great stuff that I know you are eager to get to, but indulge me for a moment, will you? Thanks.

I'm gonna spit some truths now.

95% of professional writers don't make a living at it. That's the reality. And it is one reason I'm prolific. I have to crank out novels to keep the lights on in the house. Same with thousands of other writers. If you plan on making a living at writing, then odds are, you will need to up your output. Even traditional publishers are looking for authors that can create a series in a short amount of time so they can release a book every quarter. It used to be one a year.

Welcome to the binge culture!

If you are reading this, then you want to know how to increase your output so you can keep up with the (majority) indie authors out there that are releasing new books every few weeks. Honestly? I'd throw my hands up in the air and quit this crazy gig if I didn't happen to be prolific. Another reason why I kept having you ask that question of yourself throughout this book. Is this really for you?

If it is, then that is awesome. All you have to do is keep on keeping on and eventually you will get the hang of writing a novel a month or every two months or whatever your life and schedule can handle.

Remember: none of this is easy!

It all takes hard work, dedication, and a never-say-die attitude. Yes, that's more motivational poster crap, but isn't that why you bought this book? So I could give you some pointers, but also tell you that you can do this? You can. Keep at it.

The only way you fail is if you quit!

One last bit of wisdom before we get into the guides. I cannot stress enough that the creative process is an ever-changing creature. It grows and develops like it has a life of its own, which in a weird way, it does. Always be thinking of how you can improve your process. You don't want to get stuck in a pattern that only realizes 75% of your true potential. With a couple of tweaks, even though it means more work up front, you could save lots of time and headaches down the line.

Explore. Revise. Rethink.

In other words: never stagnate. The publishing industry changes every few months, so be sure you are able and willing to change with it.

Cool?

Okay, time for you to check out the step-by-step guides.

A quick word on the guides:

They are simply how I go about writing my novels and how I went about writing this book. Literally, they will be bullet point steps. You've already read all the explanation and exposition. Now you can see the "roadmaps," if you will.

I hope they help.

Chapter Nine:
The Steps

I'm gonna simply lay this out for you. Like I said in the previous chapter/interlude, all the nitty gritty is in the body of this book. What I'll illustrate below are the basic steps I take to conceptualize, start, write, and finish a novel in four weeks.

Each novel has its own rhythm, so the timeframe for completing each step varies from novel to novel, but the end result is always a finished novel after four weeks.

Also, my process for writing this book was WAY different than writing a novel. The steps for writing non-fiction include a lot more prep and research. But, since a writing guide has a smaller word count, the actual writing part was considerably shorter and easier.

Ready?

Away we go!

Jake's Steps To Writing A Novel

I.	Come up with idea. This part is happening while I write the current novel.
II.	Do any research needed. Same with above, this part overlaps while working on a different novel.
III.	Figure out the first scene in order to hook the reader.
IV.	Create the description document for characters/objects/settings and the book description.
V.	Write the book description.
VI.	Start writing the book.
VII.	Keep writing the book.
VIII.	Finish writing the book.
IX.	First editing pass on the screen. Add page numbers.
X.	Print out manuscript.
XI.	Red pen edit time.
XII.	Enter edits into manuscript.
XIII.	Fix/adjust book description.
XIV.	Send manuscript off to publisher.
XV.	Start it all again!

Jake's Steps To Writing This Book

I.   Think hard on whether or not to write this book in the first place.

XVI.   Get a kick in the ass from my friend, and fellow writer, Patrick E. McLean.

XVII.   Realize I need to write this book.

XVIII.   Start brainstorming my ass off.

XIX.   Create an outline.

XX.   Scrap the outline and write six pages of points I'd like to include in the book.

XXI.   Create chapter headings.

XXII.   Assign a chapter number to each of the points I have on those six pages of pure chaos.

XXIII.   Write chapter headings on notecards.

XXIV.   Write every individual point on notecards.

XXV.   Clear kitchen table and set up chapter heading notecards.

XXVI.   Line up each point under their respective chapter heading (which is why I assigned chapter numbers to each point).

XXVII.   Create new outline based on the layout of the notecards.

XXVIII.   Start writing book.

XXIX.   Use the outline extensively to keep me on track and productive.

XXX.   Adjust outline as I go by combining points or by tossing points out the window due to redundancy or I simply couldn't figure out what to write.

XXXI.   Take notes as I write.

XXXII.   Use notes to punch up points.

XXXIII.   Decide to ads this step-by-step guide.

XXXIV.   Finish this step-by-step guide.

XXXV.   Do a screen edit.

XXXVI.   Print manuscript and do a red pen edit.

XXXVII.   Send off to alpha readers.

XXXVIII.   Enter suggested edits into manuscript. Or not.

XXXIX. Hand manuscript to editor. Who happens to be my wife since she is an amazing editor when it comes to essays and non-fiction writing. Thanks, babe!

XL. Rejoice that the book is finished! Huzzah!

Chapter Ten:
The Last And Final Words

Thank you!

Seriously, a huge thank you for taking the time to purchase and read this book. I truly hope I have helped you on your quest to becoming a prolific writer. It isn't an easy road to travel, but damn if it isn't fun. You may not always make enough money to support yourself, especially with the ups and downs inherent to the publishing industry, but you will get to write all those amazing ideas I know you have in that noggin of yours.

And, you know what? Now seems like the perfect time to say something that will blow your mind!

None of this is easy!

You can only fail if you quit!

I'd put a winky face emoji here, but I have no idea how to format one in an eBook. So I'll just say winky face.

Winky face!

Cheers, y'all, and happy writing!

PS- Why do you want to be prolific? Ha! Sorry. I couldn't help myself.

About The Author

Born Jacob David Bible pre-Microsoft in Bellevue, WA, Jake was whisked away to the Beaver State when he was three and raised fundamentalist pagan. Fed a steady diet of Doritos, Fritos Bean Dip, and Chinese herbal tonics, Jake had so many vivid hallucinations that he was writing and binding his own books by fifth grade.

True story.

He grew up fascinated with the speculative and the macabre. He spent many summers on his grandparent's lake reading a leather bound, Franklin Library Edition of The Tales of Edgar Allan Poe. No, it wasn't a haunted book. And, no, it wasn't a haunted lake. Yes, his grandparents were actually re-animated corpses that had been accidentally murdered and then raised from the dead when a cocktail party got just a little out of hand. And they drank gin and tonics.

True story.

Bram Stoker Award nominated-novelist, short story writer, independent screenwriter, podcaster, and inventor of the Drabble Novel, Jake has entertained thousands with his horror and sci/fi tales. He reaches audiences of all ages with his uncanny ability to write a wide range of characters and genres. Jake is the author of the bestselling *Z-Burbia* series set in Asheville, NC, the bestselling *Salvage Merc One* series, the space crime *Roak: Galactic Bounty Hunter* series, the groundbreaking Apex Trilogy (*DEAD MECH, The Americans, Metal and Ash*) and the *Mega* series for Severed Press, as well as the YA zombie novel, *Little Dead Man*, the Teen horror novel, *Intentional Haunting*, the middle grade Sci-Fi/horror *ScareScapes* series, and the *Reign of Four* series, which he calls "medieval space fiction," for Permuted Press. As of 2017, he also publishes with Bell Bridge Books and has released three books, including *Stone Cold Bastards* and the urban fantasy series *Black Box Inc.*

Jake currently lives in the Asheville, NC area with his wife, two kids, and two dogs. And although he writes about zombies and cannibals, Jake does not eat of the flesh himself (that means he's a vegetarian). But, he will eat the non-homicidal animal foodstuffs because pizza is its own food group and soy cheese just ain't gonna cut it.

True story.

75

You can reach Jake at the following:

Website: jakebible.com

Email: jakebiblefiction@gmail.com

Twitter: @jakebible

Made in the USA
Middletown, DE
17 July 2023

35339921R00046